P9-CLS-582

# AND THE CROWD GOES WILD

## Relive The Most Celebrated Sporting Events Ever Broadcast

**Joe Garner** ▪ **Bob Costas** ▪ **Hank Aaron** ▪ **Wayne Gretzky**

*Narration*        *Foreword*        *Afterword*

SOURCEBOOKS, INC.
NAPERVILLE, ILLINOIS

Copyright © 1999 by Joe Garner
Foreword Copyright © 1999 by Henry Aaron
Afterword Copyright © 1999 by Wayne Gretzky
Cover Copyright © 1999 by Sourcebooks, Inc.

*Front cover photos, clockwise from upper left:* Corbis/Bettmann, Corbis/Wally McNamee, UPI/Corbis-Bettmann, Agence France Presse/Corbis-Bettmann, Corbis/Bettmann
*Foreword photo* (Henry Aaron, page x): AP/Wide World Photos
*Afterword photo* (Wayne Gretzky): Karl Richter
*Author photo* (Joe Garner): Sandy Speer
*Back cover photos, top to bottom:* Corbis/Bettmann, AP/Wide World Photos, Reuters/Mike Blake

Audio Credits, Photo Credits, and Copyrights at back

Major League Baseball and Minor League Baseball trademarks and copyrights are used with permission of Major League Baseball Properties, Inc.

NHL and NHL trademarks are the property of the NHL and its teams. © NHL 1999. All rights reserved.

All rights reserved. No part of this book may be reproduced in any form or by any electronic or mechanical means including information storage and retrieval systems—except in the case of brief quotations embodied in critical articles or reviews—without permission in writing from its publisher, Sourcebooks.

Published by Sourcebooks, Inc.
P.O. Box 4410
Naperville, IL 60567-4410
630.961.3900
Fax: 630.961.2168

**Library of Congress Cataloging-in-Publication Data**
Garner, Joe.
  And the crowd goes wild: relive the most celebrated sporting events ever broadcast / Joe Garner.
    p.  cm.
  ISBN 1-57071-460-6 (hardcover: alk. paper)
  1. Sports—History. 2. Radio broadcasting of sports—United States. I. Title.
GV576.G335   1999
070.4'49796'0973—dc21         99-17018
                 CIP

Printed and bound in the United States of America
QG 10 9 8 7 6 5 4 3

This book is dedicated to my wife Colleen.
While her love, support, and sacrifice throughout this project may not be visible
on a single page, without it, there never could have been a book.

"And the crowd goes wild!"

# Table of Contents

# And The Crowd Goes Wild

# Introduction

In the history of sports, there are a few events that are legendary, identifiable by a simple two- or three-word phrase or even a single number: "The Called Shot," "The Catch," "The Hail Mary," "The Immaculate Reception," and "Number 715." Just mention these to any sports fan worth their TV remote and subscription to *Sports Illustrated* and they know where they were when they saw it or heard about it.

This book and CD compilation is a collection of magical moments from this hallowed category of events. They are spine-tingling outcomes: the buzzer beaters, the last-second goals, the stunning upsets, the come-from-behind victories. Moreover, this collection tells the stories behind them. These are moments that we hold in such regard and remember with such clarity, it's as if they happened only yesterday.

In some instances these events are the realization of lifelong pursuits of excellence. In others, they are simply a singular fateful moment in time when all the right elements aligned. Michael Jordan winning his sixth NBA championship on his final career basket was one of many breathtaking moments in his incredible career. Yet, for Olympic runner Billy Mills, winning the 10,000-meter gold medal at the 1964 Tokyo Games, and beating his own personal best by an astonishing forty-five seconds, was a moment in his life that would go unduplicated.

And golfer Jack Nicklaus, whose championship days were thought to be past him at age forty-six, became an inspiration when he overcame self-doubt and younger, stronger competition to win the 1986 Masters Tournament. In every instance, it's the human story that makes these moments so compelling to us.

This book is also a tribute to the sportscasters, the play-by-play guys, the storytellers in the booth who give voice to our exhilaration in victory and to our disappointment in defeat. It may be my broadcasting background, but I believe that a large part of why we remember these extraordinary athletic moments is due to the way we heard them. These talented broadcasters have provided a dramatic soundtrack to the moments we hold in almost magical regard.

Who can separate the memory of Bobby Thomson's miraculous "Shot Heard 'Round the World" from the genuine, raw excitement of Russ Hodges' lyrical anthem, "The Giants win the pennant! The Giants win the pennant! The Giants win the pennant!" It was perfection in its honest emotion and complete spontaneity.

Not even Oscar-winning composer John Williams' stirring *Olympic Fanfare and Theme* could underscore the stunning victory of the 1980 U.S. Olympic hockey team at Lake Placid as well as the passionate voice of Al Michaels shouting, "Do you believe in miracles?! Yes!"

On December 20, 1980, the NBC television network opted to broadcast a Jets–Dolphins game without the benefit of announcers. The experiment failed. The network realized what the fans already knew—the announcers were invaluable. They painted pictures in our minds when radio was king, and on television, they articulate our shared emotions as we watch extraordinary moments unfold before our eyes.

It has become popular these days to rank the greatest athletes or the greatest athletic moments. My goal with this book was simply to provide you with a scrapbook of memories of some of the most remarkable events in sports, told in stories, pictures, and sound, just the way you remember them. Where they rank and how they measure up is for you to decide.

I admit that within the first minute of starting this book, one thing became glaringly apparent. I was only going to be able to scratch the surface in terms of the events included, and I apologize if I have omitted your favorite moment.

Without exception, though, these events have stood the test of time. I promise you more than a few exciting moments and I hope you enjoy reliving them all over again—or for the very first time.

# Foreword
## by Hank Aaron

Growing up in Mobile, Alabama, I didn't really know who Joe Louis was. If he had walked into our neighborhood, probably nobody on my block would have known who he was. We didn't even know what he looked like.

But we knew Louis was black and we knew he was special. In those days before Jackie Robinson integrated baseball, Joe Louis was the only sports hero we had.

We felt we had to give him all the support we could. And, since we obviously couldn't afford to travel to wherever he was fighting, radio was the only way we could be in his corner.

When Louis was scheduled to fight, we started talking about it weeks in advance. On the night of the fight, we would all be crowded around the radio listening. And when he won, it was like we had all won.

One fight in particular stands out from all the others—Louis' rematch against Max Schmeling of Germany. Nobody wanted Schmeling to win because of Adolf Hitler.

We all clung to the radio that night, the only one we had in our house. Even though you could just faintly hear the announcer, we kept our ears stuck to that radio.

Radio was my only link to the world in those days because, of course, there was no television. At least not in my neighborhood.

It was through radio that I became a Cleveland Browns fan. I first started rooting for their running back, Marion Motley, as a kid, and have followed

in my hometown, the Mobile Bears, and I listened mainly to broadcasts of their games, along with the Major League Baseball Game of the Week, as often as I could.

I didn't have particular baseball heroes in those days. The names were all Greek to me. Partly, I think, I didn't relate to baseball players, even though I played the game myself, because I knew I had nothing to look forward to. There was no hope for me to play in the big leagues back then because I was black.

But that changed after Robinson became a Brooklyn Dodger in 1947. Suddenly, I had a chance to play major league baseball. Because of Robinson, I had a chance to have the same dreams and fantasies other kids had.

I remember hearing Bobby Thomson's pennant-winning home run against the Dodgers over the radio while coming home from school in Mobile. If there was ever an example of how broadcasts can excite and influence you, that one was it. I was so fired up that I ran home and jumped on an imaginary home plate while my imaginary teammates congratulated me.

the team ever since, the excitement of those broadcasts remaining with me into adulthood.

I am such a fan that, before the team moved to Baltimore, I disguised myself with an old hat, an overcoat, and a pair of sunglasses on several occasions and went to the Browns' home games in secret.

I sat in the "Dawg Pound" in the end zone with the hardcore fans. It was great because nobody recognized me. I enjoyed relaxing instead of being a stuffed shirt. There was nobody to bring me a beer. I got my own.

It was also through radio that I first started following baseball. The Dodgers had a minor league team

Little did I imagine that, thirty years later, I would be the center of attention on national broadcasts as I chased Babe Ruth's career home run record.

And now, a quarter of a century after I hit my 715th career home run off Al Downing of the Dodgers to pass Ruth, it seems like I still see that moment on tape everywhere I go.

Although several announcers worked that game, it is the voice of Milo Hamilton that I identify with that moment. His is the voice I always seem to hear when I see myself take that record-breaking swing.

I've had enough chill bumps from that night to last me a long time, but I still think about it all the time, although not nearly as often as I used to. It seems like a long, long time ago, even though it has only been just over twenty-five years.

Although I watch a lot of sporting events on television, I don't usually pay much attention to the announcers. I'm focused on the athletes and what makes the best ones so excellent.

But Vin Scully of the Dodgers is the one I would put at the top as far as announcing. He is a very gifted man. We have four very good announcers in Atlanta doing the Braves' games, but Scully is so knowledgeable about the game because he has been around so long. He doesn't tell a lot of jokes. He just says things that interest people.

Scully also knows exactly what pitch was thrown. What bothers me when I watch a game is an announcer who might say a pitch was a curveball when I know it was a fastball, or who might say it was low when I know it was high. But not Scully.

Since I've retired, I've had more time to watch all sports on television, so this book brought back a lot of good memories. I know that everyone who opens it will find a favorite of their own. Some may even remember my record-breaking home run. It's a great honor to have a place among all these great broadcast moments in sports history.

Perhaps just as important, it's a thrill for me to be in the company of Joe Louis, who once inspired an impressionable kid in Mobile through the magic and the power of the airwaves.

*Hank Aaron*

# AND THE CROWD GOES WILD

## GOES WILD

Relive The Most Celebrated
Sporting Events Ever Broadcast

"I looked out at center field and I pointed. I said, 'I'm going to hit the next pitched ball right past the flagpole!'"

Babe Ruth

# Babe Ruth
# Calls His Shot

George Herman "Babe" Ruth had been in the major leagues nineteen years and was already an American legend by the time his New York Yankees faced the Chicago Cubs in the 1932 World Series. That showdown was his 10th World Series and would become his seventh championship. Along the way, he hit fifteen Series home runs, but none would be as famous as his last, the "Called Shot."

Adding further intrigue to the moment was the bad blood between the Cubs and Yankees. Yankees manager Joe McCarthy had coached the Cubs to the National League pennant three years earlier. But in 1930, Cubs management unceremoniously fired him because Chicago had finished in second place. A win in the '32 Series would allow McCarthy to revel in a New York victory and exact revenge on his former employer.

Another issue fanning the flames was the Cubs' acquisition of ex-Yankees shortstop Mark Koenig, who proved to be a vital component in their pennant win. But since he'd come to the Cubs late in the season, Koenig's Chicago teammates voted to award him only one-half of the playoff bonus they received. Koenig's friends from his former team, including the outspoken Ruth, publicly blasted the Cubs and all of Chicago for the players' decision. By the time the Series moved to Chicago on October 1, the fervent Cubs fans and media were waiting for Ruth.

Game three of the series played out before a Wrigley Field crowd of fifty-one thousand fans, including New York governor and presidential candidate Franklin Delano Roosevelt. In the top of the first inning, the Yankees put two men on base and Babe Ruth walked to the plate. He was greeted by a roar of catcalls and booing from the Chicago fans and players. He smiled grimly, dug in, and parked the 2-0 pitch deep into the right center field stands, putting the Yankees in the lead 3 to 0.

The Cubs battled their way back, and in the fourth inning, tied the game at four. In the top of the fifth, Ruth was the second batter. As he stepped to the batters box, the crowd and the Cubs' dugout did their best to throw him off stride—Ruth later remembered being called "big belly" and "baboon." The taunting escalated and Ruth gave as well as he got, shouting back at the Chicago faithful and the Cubs' bench. Ruth settled into the batters box and watched as

*(left to right) Babe Ruth ■ Yankee teammates congratulate Ruth as he crosses home plate after a 1932 World Series home run.*

Cubs pitcher Charlie Root threw four pitches, running the count to two balls and two strikes—Ruth never lifted the bat from his shoulder. And then came the magical gesture. Looking at Root, Ruth held his right arm out and pointed two fingers towards center field.

There is no official film—only a distant, grainy home movie of the event—and interpretations of the specific intent of the gesture vary. Some witnesses, mostly Cubs fans and players, say Ruth was counting off the strikes and held up two fingers, indicating two strikes. Pitcher Charlie Root said

*The controversy over whether Ruth really called his shot has never been settled, as Ruth himself changed his story several times. This amateur film is the only documentation of the event. In the top photo, Ruth appears to point towards center field.*

later that if he thought Ruth was signaling an intended home run, he would have come off the
mound and "knocked him on his fanny."

But the legend is that Ruth was telling the Cubs
and their fans exactly where he was going to pound
the next pitch.

Whatever the interpretation, there's no doubt
what happened next. Root threw the ball down the
middle and Ruth blasted it deep into the center
field stands, right where he'd pointed. Some say
that home run was the longest ever hit at Wrigley
Field. Tom Manning, calling the game over radio,
shouted, "The ball is going, going, going, high into
the center field stands…and it is a home run!" The
Yankees won the game and went on to sweep the
series in four straight games.

After the game, Ruth cemented the lore of the
moment, telling reporters, "Well, I looked out at
center field and I pointed. I said, 'I'm going to hit
the next pitched ball right past the flagpole!' Well,
the Good Lord must have been with me."

*(top to bottom) The stands of Wrigley
Field were packed for game three of the
1932 World Series.* ■ *Cubs pitcher
Charlie Root* ■ *The "Sultan of
Swat" in 1931*

"Jesse Owens starts moving. He's a yard or two out in front!"

# Jesse Owens Wins Four Gold Medals

Jesse Owens did not sneak up on the track and field world in the 1936 Berlin Olympics. One year earlier, on May 25, 1935, at the collegiate Big Ten Track and Field Championships, Owens had the greatest day in track and field history, breaking three world records and tying another, not just in one day, but in less than one hour. In just forty-five minutes, he tied the world record in the 100-yard dash, then broke the world record in the 220-yard dash, the long jump, and the 220-yard hurdles. With numerous records in his name, Owens was expected to perform well at the Olympics.

Though he may have been a favorite of American sports fans and many German citizens, Owens certainly did not have the respect of the host country's officials. The stands on August 3, 1936, were teeming with Nazi supporters in Adolf Hitler's pre-war Germany. To them, Owens' athletic ability—his mere presence at "their" games—threatened their ideas of Aryan supremacy. None of this fazed the determined Owens. He not only won his first event, the 100-meter dash, but tied the Olympic record with a time of 10.3 seconds.

To no one's surprise, Hitler made no move to congratulate Owens on his victory as he had other champions. Owens made little of the apparent slight, later remarking that he hadn't been asked to shake hands with his own country's President Franklin Roosevelt either.

Owens' next event was the long jump, the event in which he held the world record. But he fouled on his first two qualifying jumps, and if he fouled on his third, he would fail to qualify for the final round. Before his final jump, German long jumper Luz Long advised Owens to start his jump well behind the take-off board, giving him enough room to legitimately jump a qualifying distance. It was a courageous move by Long to even speak with Owens in full view of Hitler and Nazi officials. Owens followed Long's advice and qualified for the finals. He won his second gold medal on his final jump with an Olympic record leap of 26 feet 5½ inches. The first person to greet Owens after his record-length jump was Long, who finished second.

On the next day of competition, Owens won his third gold medal and set another Olympic record, winning the 200-meter dash in just 20.7 seconds.

*(left to right) Jesse Owens sprints to a gold medal in the 100-meter dash.*
■ *Owens smiles before a competition in the '36 Olympics.*

He received his fourth and final medal of the '36 Olympics for the 4 x 100-meter relay. He and teammates Ralph Metcalfe, Foy Draper, and Frank Wykoff broke the world record with a time of 39.8 seconds and claimed the gold.

Upon his return to the U.S., Owens was given a hero's welcome, but the celebration was soured by the reality of segregation. He was honored with a party at New York's Waldorf-Astoria Hotel, but was made to ride in the hotel's freight elevator. In lieu of being offered lucrative endorsement deals immediately following his Olympic success, Owens earned a living by running in exhibition races, including a few with dogs and horses as competitors. He shrugged off the indignity, saying, "I had four gold medals, but you can't eat four gold medals."

But in 1950, Jesse Owens began receiving the acclaim he deserved when an Associated Press poll voted him the greatest track and field star for the first half of the twentieth century. A year later, he was invited back to Berlin to be honored at a track meet. He wore his Olympic running suit and jogged a victory lap around the stadium where he was cheered wildly by the crowd of seventy-five thousand people. Four years after his death in March 1980, a street in Berlin was renamed for the Olympic hero.

In 1990, Jesse Owens received the highest U.S. accolade when President George Bush posthumously awarded him the Congressional Gold Medal for his "unrivaled athletic triumph, but more than that, a triumph for all humanity."

*(opposite page, top to bottom) Owens extends his lead in a 200 meters heat. He later broke the world record in the 200-meter dash. ■ Despite almost not qualifying for the finals, Owens wins his second gold medal in the long jump with a distance of 26 feet 5½ inches.*

*(top to bottom) The record-breaking American 400-meter relay team. From left: Jesse Owens, Ralph Metcalfe, Foy Draper, Frank Wykoff. ■ Owens races his way to victory in the '36 Olympics.*

“The fight is over on
a technical knockout!
Max Schmeling is
beaten in one round!”

# Joe Louis Knocks Out Max Schmeling

Joe Louis Barrow became simply "Joe Louis" while filling out an application for one of his first amateur boxing bouts. He wrote so large that he could only fit his first and middle names in the space provided. Louis went on to hold one of sports' most treasured titles, that of world heavyweight champion, longer than anyone else—twelve consecutive years. Although he successfully defended his title a record twenty-five times, two fights shaped Louis into the legend he would become, and both bouts were against German boxer Max Schmeling.

In June of 1936, Louis was twenty-two years old. He carried a perfect ring record of twenty-seven wins and no losses with twenty-three knockouts. He was not yet the heavyweight champion, but the media recognized him as the most powerful force in boxing. Most boxing experts figured it was only a matter of time before Louis would win the title.

Schmeling was the former world heavyweight champion, and at age thirty, was fighting his way back into the spotlight. On June 19, 1936, the two fighters met in the ring at Yankee Stadium in New York. Louis was a substantial favorite, but unsubstantiated rumors circulated among the press that he wasn't training hard enough for the fight and wasn't in adequate shape. In the fourth round, Schmeling hit Louis with a series of punches. Finally, a hard right to Louis' chin knocked him down for the first time in his career. Louis recovered, but not fully.

Schmeling continued to pound a semiconscious Louis for eight more rounds before winning with a 12th-round knockout. The "invincible" Joe Louis had been knocked out. Schmeling, upon returning to Germany on board the zeppelin Hindenberg, was given a hero's welcome and was invited to dine with German dictator Adolf Hitler. Joe Louis vowed to win the heavyweight title but said he would never consider himself champion until he beat Schmeling.

One year later, Joe Louis won the heavyweight title by beating James J. Braddock, and one year after that, he got his rematch with Schmeling. This time, Louis was a fighter with a score to settle. He was two years older, more experienced, and in the best fighting shape of his life. Schmeling also had

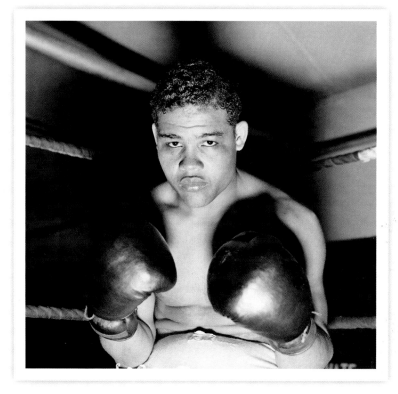

*(left to right) Schmeling's corner throws in a white towel to signify the German fighter's surrender to Louis in their 1938 rematch.* ■ *Joe Louis*

(above) Louis lost to Schmeling in a 12th-round knockout in June 1936.

maintained his strength, though he fled war-torn Europe to do so. He trained for six weeks before the fight in upstate New York, free from distracting reports of German aggression and Nazi atrocities.

The media hyped the fight with Louis as the good American and Schmeling as a symbol of the Nazi regime. It was nation against nation as each fighter received encouragement from his country's leader— Louis from President Franklin Delano Roosevelt, Schmeling from Hitler.

As Schmeling made his way into New York's Yankee Stadium on the night of June 22, 1938, he was pelted by banana peels, paper cups, and other trash. Louis entered the ring to the deafening cheers of more than seventy thousand fans.

Schmeling answered the first-round bell with a crucial tactical error. He wanted to start slow and

see what Louis' strategy would be so he could adjust his positioning. But Louis came at Schmeling and started pounding right away. Relentlessly, he threw hard punches with both hands that connected time after time. Overhand rights to Schmeling's chin dazed him. Louis moved in for more, even breaking a vertebra in his opponent's back.

Schmeling tried to counterpunch, but it was too late. The damage was done. Schmeling went to the canvas. He got up, but soon went down again on all fours after a vicious combination by Louis. Schmeling rose again, but was put face-down on the canvas with a right to the jaw. This time, referee Arthur Donovan stopped the fight, just 2:04 into the first round. Joe Louis now had his revenge with a first-round knockout of Max Schmeling.

Ringside reporters called it one of the most savage beatings ever witnessed in boxing. Schmeling spent

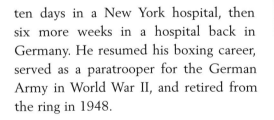

ten days in a New York hospital, then six more weeks in a hospital back in Germany. He resumed his boxing career, served as a paratrooper for the German Army in World War II, and retired from the ring in 1948.

In America, Joe Louis was a hero. He retained the world heavyweight title for nearly eleven more years. During World War II he fought exhibition bouts and donated two championship purses to the war effort. He put his boxing career on hold for three years when he enlisted in the army in 1942. Louis died of a heart attack on April 12, 1981, and at the request of President Ronald Reagan, he was buried in Arlington National Cemetery in Washington, D.C., a final resting place of honor reserved for American heroes.

*(above) Louis exacts revenge over Schmeling by knocking him out in one round in June 1938.* ■ *(left) Louis on duty as a U.S. Army soldier in 1942*

"Today, I consider myself the luckiest man on the face of the earth."
Lou Gehrig

# Lou Gehrig Says Good-bye

On July 4, 1939, Shirley Povich, a *Washington Post* reporter, wrote, "I saw strong men weep this afternoon." That was the day Lou Gehrig bid farewell to baseball. To this day, Gehrig's simple, heartfelt speech remains the most memorable farewell ever uttered by an athlete.

Lou Gehrig was the only surviving child of German immigrant parents. He first showed signs of his baseball prowess while in high school. After graduation, Gehrig enrolled at Columbia University. But baseball beckoned, and in the summer of 1923 he signed a $3,500 contract with the New York Yankees. In his sixteen seasons as a Yankee, the man nicknamed the "Iron Horse" played in 2,164 games, and in doing so he set one of sports' most enduring records—2,130 of those games were played consecutively. It is a record that stood for over fifty years, until modern-day iron man Cal Ripken Jr. passed the mark in 1995.

By the end of the 1938 season, Gehrig had led the Yankees to three straight World Series titles, but there were signs that the Iron Horse was beginning to falter. He had twenty-nine home runs, 114 RBIs, and batted .295—above average for a normal player, but Gehrig's worst season in twelve years. Everybody chalked it off as a slump. But when the '39 season started, things grew worse. Gehrig was having trouble just swinging the bat, and his physical coordination was off. No one knew it then, but medical tests would later prove that he had amyotrophic lateral sclerosis—a disorder in which messages from the brain never reach the muscles, resulting in paralysis and eventual death. It was a disorder that would first take Gehrig's career, then his life, and finally his name: "Lou Gehrig's Disease."

By late April 1939, Gehrig was in bad shape. He could not hit, and he was having trouble playing his position. On April 30, in what would be his final game, Gehrig went hitless for the fifth time in eight games. Gehrig was a fierce competitor, but he was also a team player, and he didn't want to hurt the Yankees' chances. On May 2, 1939, Gehrig, the team's captain, approached manager Joe McCarthy and asked to be taken out of the lineup. McCarthy offered token resistance, and finally relented. Gehrig's streak came to an end.

As captain, it was Gehrig's duty to present the starting lineup to the head umpire. Once he did, an announcement came over the stadium's public address system. "Ladies and gentlemen, this is the first time Lou Gehrig's name will not appear on the Yankee lineup in 2,130 consecutive games."

*(left to right) Lou Gehrig stands with head bowed and gifts at his feet as Master of Ceremonies Sid Mercer speaks at Lou Gehrig Day in front of a sell-out crowd at Yankee Stadium.*
■ *Gehrig attempts to hold back tears during his tribute on July 4, 1939.*

The small Detroit crowd gave Gehrig a standing ovation. He turned and walked back into the Yankee dugout. Then, he sat on a corner of the bench and tears welled in his eyes.

On June 19, 1939, Gehrig's 36th birthday, he received the results of tests he had undergone at the Mayo Clinic. They confirmed his condition as incurable. The following July 4, the Yankees declared it Lou Gehrig Day, so the stricken ballplayer donned the Yankee pinstripes once again. There was a double-header that day, and the ceremony was held between games. The team was retiring Lou Gehrig's number, making him the very first major league player to be so honored. Among those in attendance were Gehrig's teammates from past seasons, including Babe Ruth and others from the legendary 1927 New York Yankees. In addition, members of the stadium's grounds crew, the hot dog vendors, and fans crowded the stadium with gifts.

*(clockwise) Gehrig bats for Columbia University. ■ The Iron Horse during his sixteen-season career with the Yankees ■ Gehrig in 1923*

New York Mayor Fiorello LaGuardia and the Postmaster General spoke. Then, Coach McCarthy stepped to the microphone and described Gehrig as "the finest example of a ballplayer, sportsman, and citizen that baseball has ever known." He could control his emotions no longer. Openly weeping, he turned to Gehrig and said, "Lou, what else can I say except that it was a sad day in the life of everybody who knew you when you came into my hotel room that day in Detroit and told me you were quitting as a ballplayer because you felt yourself a hindrance to the team. My God, man, you were never that."

With the tributes, honors, and gifts distributed, there was no one left to speak but Gehrig himself. But, for a moment, it didn't seem like it would happen. Master of Ceremonies Sid Mercer looked over at Gehrig, and saw him breaking down, obviously too choked up to speak. Turning to the fans, he said, "I shall not ask Lou Gehrig to make a speech. I do not believe that I should."

And with that, the crew started to take away the microphones. Gehrig appeared to be headed off the field, and the ceremony seemed to be over. But then, he turned back and stepped up to the microphone. He held up his hand to the crowd for quiet. A hush fell over Yankee Stadium, and Gehrig began to speak. In proclaiming himself the "luckiest man on the face of the earth," Lou Gehrig made a farewell to baseball that will remain one of the most remembered moments in all of sports.

### Lou Gehrig's Career Statistics

| | |
|---|---|
| **Batting Average** | .340 |
| **Hits** | 2,721 |
| **Home Runs** | 493 |
| **RBIs** | 1,991 |
| **Consecutive Games Played** | 2,130 |

*(above) Babe Ruth, right, embraces his former teammate during Gehrig's farewell ceremony.*

"The Giants win the pennant!
The Giants win the pennant!"

Russ Hodges

# Bobby Thomson Hits
# "Shot Heard 'Round the World"

It was the playoffs of 1951. An American Dream played out on a baseball field with all the story ingredients Americans loved—the underdog; an ordinary man who beat the odds, rose to a challenge, and became a hero; and, of course, it all happened at the last possible moment.

The buildup began in August. At that time, the Brooklyn Dodgers had a comfortable lead in the National League pennant race—enough so that their crosstown rivals, the New York Giants, were counted out easily. They were 13½ games behind the Dodgers. With forty-four games to go, it seemed impossible for the Giants to catch up.

But after August 11, the Giants won thirty-seven of the remaining forty-four games, rivaling the Dodgers' twenty-four wins. Near the end of the season, the Giants actually caught and passed the Dodgers, but only for a matter of hours. The Giants won an afternoon contest and went up a half game, only to have the Dodgers come back and tie the race the same evening.

On the very last day of the regular season, the Giants were, once again, a half game ahead and awaiting results of the Dodgers–Philadelphia Phillies match-up. It was a nailbiter. The extra-inning game set a New York playoff into motion when the Dodgers' Jackie Robinson hit a 14th-inning home run to win.

The National League best-of-three playoff series began in the Dodgers' home park of Ebbets Field. Undeterred by the devoted hometown fans, the Giants embarrassed their competition on its own turf, winning easily, 3 to 1. The second game was at the Polo Grounds, the Giants' home field. The Dodgers repaid the Giants for the defeat they had suffered by soundly beating them 10 to 0 to take game two. The series was tied, and down to one game for the right to face another New York team, the Yankees, in the World Series.

The final game was tight—tied at 1 into the eighth inning. The Dodgers' bats caught fire against Giants pitcher Sal Maglie, and they finished the inning with a 4 to 1 lead. Though the Dodgers did not score in the top of the ninth, they were still up three runs and were just three outs away from championship play.

In the last half of the last inning, the Giants were up against one of the most feared pitchers in baseball, Don Newcombe. Before the Giants pushed a run over in the seventh, he'd pitched twenty consecutive scoreless innings.

And then, in front of more than thirty-four thousand paying fans and a national television and radio

*(left to right) The Giants' Bobby Thomson hits his famous home run. The dotted line indicates the path of the ball.*
■ *Thomson hits the "Shot Heard 'Round the World."*

 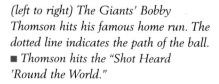

audience, momentum swung the Giants' way. Alvin Dark came up first and singled. Don Mueller followed with another single while Dark took third. There were men on first and third with nobody out. Hope glimmered in the Polo Grounds. The tying run was at the plate.

Newcombe got the next batter, Monte Irvin, out on a weak pop-up to Gil Hodges behind first base. Dodgers manager Charley Dressen walked to the mound, conferred with his future Hall of Fame pitcher, and decided to leave him in the game. There was one down and just two more outs and the National League pennant would belong to Brooklyn.

Giants first baseman Whitey Lockman stepped to the plate. He hit a double, scoring Alvin Dark from third. Don Mueller surged towards third and slid. He was safe, but his ankle was seriously injured and he couldn't stand on it. He was carried off the field on a stretcher.

*(top to bottom) Thomson runs past fans on his way to the locker room after his home run. ■ Thomson is mobbed by teammates following his pennant-winning home run. ■ Giants fans raise Thomson onto their shoulders.*

With New York now posing a serious threat, Dressen pulled Newcombe and replaced him with Ralph Branca. Branca finished his warm-up pitches and Bobby Thomson, the outfielder and third baseman nicknamed the "Staten Island Scot," stepped into the batters box.

Giants announcer Russ Hodges described the scene on radio, "Hartung down the line at third, not taking any chances. Lockman without too big a lead at second, but he'll be running like the wind if Thomson hits one." Thomson took Branca's first pitch, "It's strike one off the knees!" as Hodges called it. Thomson dug in. Branca pitched again, and this time Thomson swung and connected, sending a low-flying line drive toward the left field seats. It cleared Dodgers left fielder Andy Pafko's outstretched glove and flew over the fence 315 feet away from home plate.

Almost hysterical, Hodges screamed out the simple declarative sentence that he would repeat five times—and sports fans, baseball historians, and TV retrospectives would repeat a million more. "The Giants win the pennant! The Giants win the pennant! The Giants win the pennant! The Giants win the pennant! Bobby Thomson hits into the lower deck of the left field stands! The Giants win the pennant and they're going crazy!"

First across home was Clint Hartung scoring from third base, followed by Whitey Lockman scoring from second. Finally, Thomson triumphantly crossed home plate where he was mobbed by his delirious teammates.

The home run later titled the "Shot Heard 'Round the World" saved the Giants that day and set Thomson's name in the history books. Although the Giants went on to lose the World Series to the Yankees, Thomson's pennant-winning home run will be forever remembered among the greatest last-minute heroics in sports history.

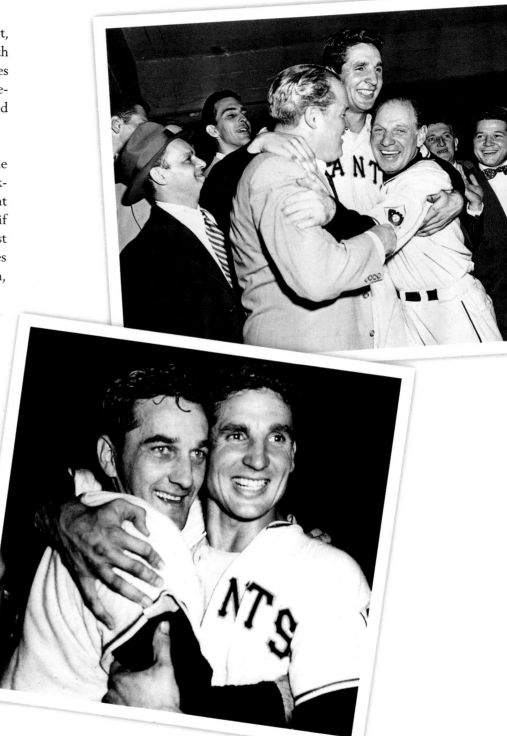

(top to bottom) Giants owner Horace Stoneham (left) and manager Leo Durocher hug Thomson. ■ Giants pitcher Larry Jansen (left) and Thomson embrace following their playoff victory.

"A perfect game by Don Larsen... Listen to this crowd roar!"

Bob Wolff

# Don Larsen Throws World Series Perfect Game

New York Yankees pitcher Don Larsen marked the middle of the twentieth century with a feat that had never happened before in baseball history, and hasn't happened since. On October 8, 1956, pitching against the Brooklyn Dodgers in the World Series, Larsen threw a perfect game, retiring twenty-seven batters in a row—no walks, no errors, no hit batsmen—no baserunners, period.

Larsen was an unlikely candidate for accomplishing the amazing feat. The twenty-seven-year-old had a respectable eleven wins versus five losses that year, but his record was nonetheless overshadowed in the Yankees rotation by stronger seasons from Whitey Ford, Johnny Kucks, and Tom Sturdivant. Plus, in the World Series, he was facing what might have been the best Dodgers team to ever play in Brooklyn, with a lineup including future Hall of Famers Jackie Robinson, Pee Wee Reese, Duke Snider, and Roy Campanella.

In game two of the series, Larsen's first appearance against the Dodgers, he was far from the perfect pitcher. In fact, Yankees manager Casey Stengel removed him from the game in the second inning after he walked four men and allowed a base hit. The Dodgers won the game 13 to 8, taking a series lead of two games to none.

But the Yankees fought back and won the next two games, tying the series. It was on to game five and one of the premier pitching performances in the history of professional baseball.

Don Larsen's less than stellar performance in game two caused him to question his pitching mechanics. He had lost his pinpoint control, and in desperation he made the drastic decision to discard his windup. Instead of using his usual windmilling arm motion and high leg kick, he just aimed the ball and fired. The change in motion would help make Larsen nearly untouchable in game five.

*(left to right) Yankees catcher Yogi Berra jumps into Don Larsen's arms just after the last batter strikes out. ■ Dodgers owner Walter O'Malley congratulates Larsen on his perfect World Series game.*

Certainly he could not have thrown his masterpiece without the superb defensive play of his Yankees teammates. Andy Carey, whom Stengel had positioned at third base, made two single-saving plays. In the second inning, the Dodgers' Jackie Robinson hit a hot grounder to Carey's left. Although Carey couldn't quite make the play himself, he was able to deflect the ball to shortstop Gil McDougald, who threw Robinson out at first. Later, Gil Hodges smashed a line drive that looked like a sure hit. Moving with the crack of the bat, Carey stuck his glove out, knocked Hodges' rocket down, and caught it before it hit the ground.

Yankees outfielder Mickey Mantle also contributed, saving at least a double by running down another Gil Hodges smash and making a one-handed catch in deep center field.

In the fourth inning, Mantle homered off Dodgers starting pitcher Sal Maglie, giving Larsen the only run he would need to win. As the game went into the sixth, seventh, and eighth innings, the crowd hung on every pitch. By the top of the ninth, they were on their feet. Bob Wolff, the sportscaster calling the game for Mutual Radio, gave voice to the excitement in the stadium, saying, "I'll guarantee

*Larsen strikes out the last batter in his perfect game against the Dodgers. He abandoned his usual windmilling windup and leg kick before the game, opting for a straightforward approach.*

that nobody but nobody has left this ballpark. And if somebody did manage to leave early, man, he is missin' the greatest."

Dodgers pinch hitter Dale Mitchell was the last batter to face Don Larsen that day. Twenty-six had come up before him, and twenty-six had gone down. He was the Dodgers' last chance. But on that October day, Don Larsen would not be denied. He struck Mitchell out on four pitches and Yankee Stadium turned to bedlam.

As Larsen's teammates rushed to congratulate him, catcher Yogi Berra would leave fans with one of the most indelible memories in all of sports. The catcher ecstatically ran to Larsen, leapt on him, wrapped his arms and legs around the pitcher and planted kisses on both of his cheeks. "Listen to this crowd roar!" Wolff cried. "A perfect performance by Don Larsen. Man! What a thrill this is!"

The Yankees went on to win the 1956 World Series 4 games to 3. To this date, Don Larsen remains one of just over a dozen pitchers to throw a perfect game, and the only one to do so in a World Series. On July 18, 1999, Larsen returned to Yankee Stadium to celebrate Yogi Berra Day, where he threw out the ceremonial first pitch to his former catcher. Larsen and Berra left some magic on the field that Sunday afternoon, then stayed on to watch from the stands. They witnessed an improbable tribute, as pitcher David Cone became the third Yankee to throw a perfect game.

*Larsen congratulates pitcher David Cone after Cone's perfect game against the Montreal Expos, July 18, 1999. Larsen had thrown out the game's first pitch to celebrate Yogi Berra Day.*

"The Colts are the world champions, Ameche scores!"

Bob Wolff

# "The Greatest Game Ever Played": Colts vs. Giants

For over four decades, sports authorities have called the 1958 NFL championship showdown between the Baltimore Colts and the New York Giants "The Greatest Game Ever Played." That game, on December 28, 1958, also marked the day America discovered the NFL, as millions of viewers tuned in on television, many for the first time.

The game was a clash of titans—the Colts, led by quarterback Johnny Unitas, were an offensive powerhouse, and the Giants boasted a terrific defense. The Giants drew first blood in the game, going up 3 to 0 in the first quarter on a Pat Summerall field goal. But the Colts scored two touchdowns before the half to go on top 14 to 3. The Colts nearly scored again in the third quarter, but were thrown for a loss at the Giants' five-yard line on fourth down. The Giants took over, and their offense drove ninety-five yards to score.

Just into the fourth quarter, the Giants scored again, taking a 17 to 14 lead on a fifteen-yard touchdown pass from Charlie Conerly to Frank Gifford. With just 1:56 left to play, the Colts got the ball back for one final drive after a Gifford run was marked short of a first down by officials.

Starting from their own fourteen-yard line, Unitas took to the air and the Colts marched down the field. With just seven seconds left, kicker Steve Myhra tied the game at 17 with a field goal, forcing the first sudden-death overtime in NFL championship history.

The Giants won the coin toss for first possession in the overtime, but after receiving, couldn't gain a first down. They punted and the Colts began their drive on their own twenty-yard line. Unitas led his team the length of the field to the one-yard line, and on third down, running back Alan Ameche bulled into the end zone to win the championship.

The game was a hit, but as fans watched the telecast on the NBC network, it almost turned to disaster when the network lost its signal just before the finish. Fortunately, an apparently drunken spectator meandered onto the field, and by the time officials corralled him, NBC had restored its picture feed. It was discovered later that the stumbling fan was actually NBC News business manager Stan Rotkiewicz, working the game as a statistician. His crafty antics may have saved the network from missing a historic finish to a remarkable game.

*(left to right) Baltimore Colts fullback Alan Ameche dives through a hole in the Giants' defensive line to score in sudden-death overtime. ■ Ameche finds his way into the end zone to win in the first overtime game in NFL championship history.*

"It's Wilma Rudolph leading all the way!"

# Wilma Rudolph Sprints to Olympic Gold

Wilma Rudolph was born prematurely on June 23, 1940, in St. Bethlehem, Tennessee, weighing only 4½ pounds. The family was poor, and her mother, Blanche, not only kept busy by tending to her twenty-one other children and cleaning the homes of wealthy families, but she also helped young Wilma through a rash of debilitating diseases. At the age of four, Wilma Rudolph's left leg and foot began to weaken and deform. She was diagnosed two years later with incurable polio and had to wear special leg braces and shoes for, according to her doctor, the rest of her life. But that doctor had underestimated the strength and willpower of the Rudolph family.

Rudolph later recalled, "My mother taught me very early to believe I could achieve anything I wanted to. The first was to walk without braces." And so, she spent the next seven years struggling to get back on her feet. After just two years, Rudolph could walk in her braces and doctors taught family members how to perform needed physical therapy. From then on, it became her siblings' job to help her. Every day, they took turns massaging their sister's crippled leg. Eventually, their determination paid off and she was soon out of the braces and making up for lost time.

She developed a passion for basketball, and after her brothers set up a hoop in the yard, they could not tear her away from it. She became so good that she not only made her high school basketball team, but became an all-state player and set a Tennessee record by scoring forty-nine points in a single game. That was when the Tennessee State track coach, Ed Temple, noticed Rudolph. While still in high school, she began attending Temple's daily college practices and competing in Amateur Athletic Union track events. At one of those events, the 1955 AAU Nationals, none other than baseball legend Jackie Robinson was so impressed by the fifteen-year-old he predicted, "One day, you're going to be the world's fastest woman." A year later, she got

*(clockwise from left) Rudolph streaks past the finish line during the first semifinal of the 100 meters. ■ Though out of leg braces, six-year-old Rudolph, right, still had years of therapy before her when she posed with her older sister Yvonne. ■ Rudolph, left, and Tennessee State teammate Mae Faggs race to the finish line of the 1960 Olympic trials.*

her first taste of Olympic competition, qualifying as a member of the U.S. 4 x 100 relay team in the 1956 Melbourne Summer Games. She came home with the bronze medal and the determination to compete again in the 1960 Games.

After graduating from high school, Rudolph received a full scholarship to attend Tennessee State. There, she was a vital member of the Lady Tigerbelles, the track team that would also comprise half the women's squad for the 1960 Summer Olympic Games held in Rome, Italy.

The first of Rudolph's three gold medals at the Rome Olympics came in her first event, the 100-meter sprint. In the semifinals, she tied the world record of 11.3 seconds. Then in the finals, she beat that mark by .3, winning the medal in eleven seconds flat. Though the record didn't stand because the wind speed was .752 meters per second over the limit, the win still made her the fastest woman in the world, proving Jackie Robinson's earlier prediction true.

Rudolph set a new Olympic record of 23.2 seconds during the first heat of the 200-meter race, and later won the gold for that event, running it in twenty-four seconds.

Her last medal came in her final event—the 4 x 100-meter relay. Her teammates were all fellow Lady Tigerbelles, a dominating force. By the third leg of the race, they had a two-yard lead over the second-place German team. With Rudolph running the anchor leg, a win seemed guaranteed. But

*(top left) Rudolph begins the 200 meters heat where she set an Olympic record of 23.2 seconds. ■ (top right) The U.S. 4 x 100 relay team. From left: Rudolph, Barbara Jones, Lucinda Williams, Martha Hudson. ■ (center) As the anchor, Rudolph wins the 4 x 100 relay semifinal. ■ (bottom) Rudolph crosses the finish line of the 100 meters to win her first Olympic gold medal.*

a fumbled baton pass between Rudolph and teammate Lucinda Williams set Rudolph off-pace. Even still, she was able to regain the lead and win the gold. With this win, Rudolph became the first female track athlete to win three gold medals for the United States.

Returning home after the Olympics, Rudolph also showed her strength of character when her hometown wanted to throw her a victory parade. The mayor was a strict segregationist and the parade was to be segregated as well. Rudolph refused to participate unless everyone could attend. The mayor acquiesced, and the subsequent parade and banquet were the first integrated events in the history of Clarksville, Tennessee.

*(top to bottom) Rudolph wins the 4 x 100 finals to earn her third gold medal.* ■ *Rudolph receives her first Olympic gold for the 100-meter dash with medalists Dorothy Hyman, left, and Giuseppina Leone, right.* ■ *Rudolph waves to a crowd of supporters at her hometown parade.*

"Williams swings and there's a long drive to deep right! That ball is going, and it is gone!"

Curt Gowdy

# Ted Williams Finishes Career with Home Run

The annals of baseball will mark the career of Ted Williams both for his perfect swing and for his distinction as the last man to hit over .400 for a single season. But perhaps more than anything else, fans of the game will remember Williams for the way he left the game, closing the door on a remarkable career on his own terms, and with one triumphant flourish.

Theodore Samuel Williams broke into professional baseball in 1936 with his hometown San Diego Padres of the Pacific Coast League. He was a tall, skinny seventeen-year-old with big talent, and it didn't take long for major league clubs to notice.

After one year with the Padres, the Boston Red Sox bought his contract for $25,000 and sent him to the Millers, their Minneapolis farm team. There, his youthful self-confidence annoyed his coach so badly that the coach went to the owner and threatened to quit if Williams was not removed from the team. The owner replied that Williams was batting .360, and if the coach chose to quit, so be it. The coach stayed, and so did Williams.

Williams was called up to the Red Sox for the 1939 season. Except for time spent as a Marine Corps pilot during World War II and the Korean War—where he flew as future astronaut John Glenn's wingman—he played his entire nineteen-season major league career in Boston.

In 1939, his rookie season, Williams batted in 145 runs for the Red Sox and became the first rookie ever to lead the league in RBIs. Two years later, he led the majors with an American League record .406 batting average. And before he left the game, he was the American League batting champion six times.

But even with all that going for him, Williams still did not get the accolades he desired. His achievements couldn't secure what Boston fans most wanted—a pennant. When his numbers dropped a few points early in the 1940 season, the press responded to the fans' scrutiny, writing that Williams did not work hard enough. He countered in an interview, stating if that was the way they were going to treat him, he'd rather be a fireman.

The next day, when he took his place in left field, the crowd booed him. Williams squared off against the fans and the press in Boston, and for the rest of his career, the stubborn slugger never backed down. That season, Williams vowed to never again

*(left to right) Ted Williams swung his bat for a home run 521 times in his nineteen-season career.* ■ *Batting practice, March 1939*

tip his cap to the fans—something he'd done with enthusiasm his first year in Boston. He kept his vow for fifty-one years. In 1991, the Red Sox threw Ted Williams Day at Fenway Park and, turning to the crowd, he dramatically tipped his cap.

Williams' last season was 1960, and his last at-bat was perhaps the most dramatic of his career. Before the team's final home game of the season on September 28, 1960, there was a small ceremony that began with a speech by longtime Red Sox announcer Curt Gowdy. "As we all know, this is the final home game for—in my opinion and most of yours—the greatest hitter who ever lived, Ted Williams," Gowdy said, later adding, "I don't know if we'll ever see another one like him."

*(left to right) Williams swings for the last time in his career, hitting his 521st home run.* ■ *Red Sox catcher Jim Pagliaroni congratulates Williams on his final home run as he crosses home plate.*

When Williams stepped up to the microphone to conclude the ceremony, he seemed to have made his peace with the fans and the press, stating that in spite of all the hardships, "baseball has been the most wonderful thing in my life. If I were starting over again and someone asked me where is the one place I would like to play, I would want it to be in Boston, with the greatest owner in baseball and the greatest fans in America. Thank you."

After a standing ovation and eight innings of play, the fans at Fenway reverently watched what was most likely Ted Williams' last at-bat. Williams stood in against Orioles pitcher Jack Fisher. Fisher blew a fastball by Williams, who swung with all his might and missed by a mile. Williams said later that he was mystified and chagrined because he had no idea where the pitch was. And at that moment, he knew he'd picked the right time to quit. But he hadn't quit yet.

Calling the game, Gowdy commented, "Everybody quiet now here at Fenway Park…knowing that this is probably his last time at bat. One out, nobody on, last of the eighth inning." Williams stood in for the third pitch and it was right down the pipe. And like he'd done 520 times before, he pushed the bat forward and smashed a line drive over the right field fence. "Williams swings and there's a long drive to deep right! That ball is going, and it is gone," shouted Gowdy. It was Williams' 521st and final home run. Gowdy, admittedly choked up as he watched Williams rounding the bases, underscored the moment by simply stating, "A home run for Ted Williams in his last time at bat in the major leagues!"

(top to bottom) Cameras snap as Williams bows his head and says good-bye to baseball. September 28, 1960 ■ During Ted Williams Day, May 12, 1991, Williams tips his hat to the crowd in Fenway Park.

"Back to the wall goes Berra.
It is over the fence!
Home run! The Pirates win!"
Chuck Thompson

# Bill Mazeroski Home Run Wins World Series

The match-up of the underdog versus the perennial powerhouse is among the most eagerly anticipated in all of sports. In 1960, the Pittsburgh Pirates played underdog to the favored New York Yankees in a World Series to remember.

It was an East Coast match-up, the rough and tumble Pittsburgh Pirates against one of baseball's most elite teams, the Yankees. The strong Yankees lineup card included such stars and sluggers as Mickey Mantle, Roger Maris (that year's MVP), Yogi Berra, Tony Kubek, and Bill "Moose" Skowron. It was an altogether awesome team, managed by Casey Stengel. The legendary manager was seventy years old, in his last season of coaching the Yankees, and shooting for a seventh World Series victory.

Pittsburgh had its stars too: Roberto Clemente; that year's National League batting champ, Dick Groat; and all-star second baseman Bill Mazeroski. But Pittsburgh's stars were nothing like the total team New York fielded, nor did they have the Yankees' incredible tradition. By 1960, the Yankees had won the World Series eighteen times, including six times in the 1950s. The Pirates hadn't even participated in one since 1927. That year, they went up against the Yankees of Babe Ruth and Lou Gehrig, a squad many consider the best major league team of all time, and were blown out in four straight games. The last time they'd actually won the World Series was in 1925.

The best-of-seven series opened at Forbes Field in Pittsburgh and the hometown underdogs struck first, surprising the confident New York team 6 to 4. But the celebration was short-lived. In games two and three, the Yankees lived up to their nickname, the Bronx Bombers, and shelled Pittsburgh, ringing up overwhelming wins of 16 to 3 and 10 to 0. It began to look like the Pirates' only glory would be their game one win.

But the Pirates wouldn't be counted out. They battled back and eked out a 3 to 2 win in game four, tying the series at two games apiece. In game five, the Pirates won another close one 5 to 2 and were just a game away from total victory. But the Yankees came back and blasted them for a third time. Game six was a 12 to 0 rout. The series was even once again. The championship was down to the final game.

Although the series was tied in games won, the Pirates had been outscored by a 47 to 16 margin. The Yankees offense had also piled up individual and team records for runs and hits in World Series play, while posting a phenomenal .341 batting average.

*(clockwise from left) Mazeroski hits home plate after securing a World Series victory for the Pirates. ■ A packed Yankee Stadium ■ A pitch is thrown at Yankee Stadium.*

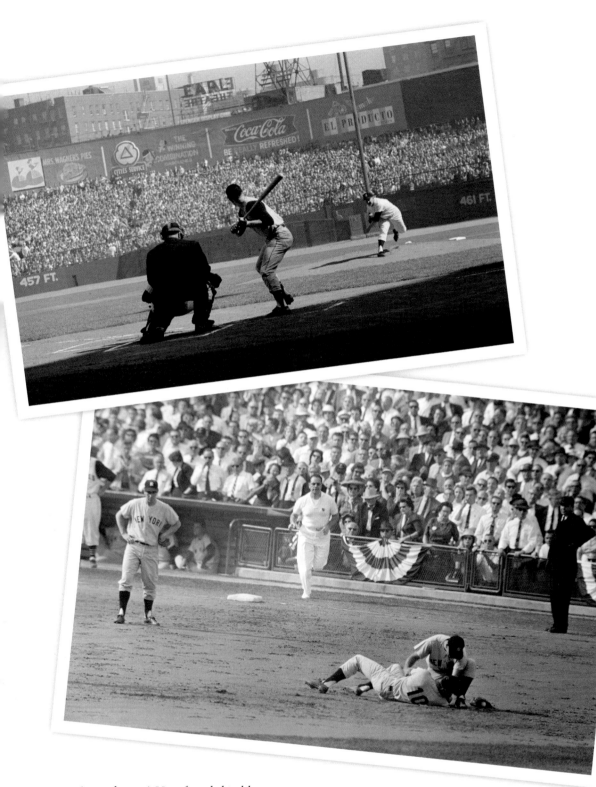

After game six, when all these numbers were run by Pirates manager Danny Murtaugh, he gave it the Pittsburgh perspective. "So far as I know, they haven't changed the World Series rules," Murtaugh said. "This thing still goes to the team that wins four games, and not to the club that makes the most records."

The last game played out in front of the underdog Pirates' home crowd. By the second inning, Pittsburgh was up 4 to 0. In the fifth, Moose Skowron homered, putting New York on the board. Then, in the sixth, the Yankee sluggers went to work, scoring four runs, including a Yogi Berra home run. The Pirates were down 5 to 4. And for good measure, the Yankees put two more runs on the board in the top of the eighth.

With New York up 7 to 4, the Pirates had only a few outs left. But, in the bottom of the eighth inning, fate dealt a stunning blow to the Yankees. The Pirates had a man on first when Bill Virdon smacked a hot grounder straight at New York shortstop Tony Kubek. It was a double play ball. But just before Kubek could scoop the ball up and toss it to second base, the ball took a bad hop and hit him in the larynx. The runners were both safe, and Kubek was loaded into an ambulance and taken to the hospital. The Pirates took advantage of the change in momentum, scoring five runs and ending the eighth with a 9 to 7 lead. The championship was just three outs away.

The see-saw scoring continued in the top of the ninth when three Yankees singles and a botched force play at first produced two New York runs and tied the score at nine runs each. In the bottom of the ninth, Pittsburgh's hometown boy Bill Mazeroski was first to bat.

Mazeroski stepped in against Yankee pitcher Ralph Terry. Terry's first pitch was a strike. His second pitch made history. Mazeroski got hold of a chest-

*(top to bottom) View from behind home plate in Yankee Stadium during the 1960 World Series ■ Yankees shortstop Tony Kubek lies on the field after being hit in the larynx by a ground ball.*

high fastball and sent it soaring over the left field wall for a 10 to 9 victory, and the first World Series championship for Pittsburgh in thirty-five years.

NBC Radio's Chuck Thompson called the game from the broadcast booth and announced the last-minute heroics. "A high-fly ball going deep to left, this may do it! Back to the wall goes Berra. It is over the fence. Home run! The Pirates win!" He became so flustered by the miraculous home run, he excitedly announced the wrong score, 10 to 0.

As Mazeroski rounded the bases toward home, the crowd at Pittsburgh's Forbes Field cheered ecstatically. They had witnessed the first series-ending home run in World Series history, launching Mazeroski to the status of legend, and the Pirates to one of the greatest underdog triumphs of all time.

*(top to bottom) Fans mob Bill Mazeroski after his game-winning home run.* ■ *Mazeroski answers press questions after a champagne dousing.* ■ *Pittsburgh holds a victory parade with Mazeroski, left, as its star.*

"It's like nothing that ever happened to me before."

Wilt Chamberlain

# Wilt Chamberlain Scores 100 Points

Heading into a late-season game against the New York Knicks, Philadelphia Warriors center Wilt Chamberlain already held the top two single-game scoring records in the NBA. In January 1962, he scored seventy-three points in a regulation forty-eight minutes and had seventy-eight points in a triple-overtime game just one month before.

With New York's star center Phil Jordan absent from the March 2, 1962, match-up, the Knicks had no one to guard the 7-foot 1-inch Chamberlain. In front of a crowd of 4,124, Chamberlain was unstoppable, scoring forty-one points by halftime and beating his previous seventy-eight-point record with 7:51 left in the game.

The fans in Hershey, Pennsylvania's Fairgrounds, the arena where the Warriors played several home games, began to chant, "Give it to Wilt," as he neared the one-hundred-point mark. The Knicks, meanwhile, fought Chamberlain's progress every step of the way, guarding him with all five players, and, each time they touched the ball, attempting to hold possession for the duration of the twenty-four-second clock.

Philadelphia responded to the Knicks' stall tactics. Warriors coach Frank McGuire sent in players from the bench to foul New York players, regain possession, and feed the ball to Chamberlain. With 1:19 left in the fourth quarter, Chamberlain's fans cheered as number ninety-eight dropped through the hoop. "Wilt the Stilt" was now only a basket away from the impossible.

The Knicks then had possession of the ball but suffered a turnover at the hands of Chamberlain, who took a shot from the foul line and missed. The next time Philadelphia had the ball, Chamberlain moved into position, but missed two consecutive shots.

The ball ended up in the hands of the Warriors' Joe Ruklick, who hurled it at the backboard where Chamberlain caught the ball and slammed it through the net. The crowd, already on its feet, ran on to the court to celebrate even though time remained on the clock. Chamberlain walked to the locker room, smiling all the way. After a five-minute delay to clear the court—and the forty-six seconds left in regulation play—the Warriors beat the Knicks 169 to 147.

Wilt Chamberlain, normally a 51 percent free-throw shooter, had made twenty-eight of thirty-two shots from the foul line and hit thirty-six of sixty-three from the field. In each quarter, he never shot less than 50 percent. He admitted, "It's like nothing that ever happened to me before."

*(left to right) Chamberlain holds a sign reading "100" after scoring one hundred points against the Knicks. ■ Chamberlain sinks his 100th point.*

"What a tremendous surprise here! Bill Mills of the United States wins the 10,000 meter!"

Bud Palmer

# Billy Mills Wins 10,000-Meter Gold

**M**ost athletes spend countless hours perfecting their skills, slowly building to their peak performance. But in the 1964 Tokyo Olympics, Billy Mills hit his peak in the biggest contest of his athletic career, improving his own personal best time by such an astonishing amount he not only shocked himself, but also shocked the world.

No American had ever won the 10,000-meter Olympic gold medal, and no one even considered Mills would come close. His best time at the 10,000 meters was 29 minutes 10 seconds, almost one full minute slower than the world record held by Olympic competitor Ron Clarke of Australia. In fact, many of the thirty-seven runners entered in the October 14 race had better personal best times than Mills.

The race started and Clarke took the early lead. He was chased by previous Olympians Petr Bolotnikov of Russia and Murray Hallberg of New Zealand, and future Olympic medalists Mamo Wolde of Ethiopia and Mohamed Gammoudi of Tunisia. Mills managed to keep pace with the chase pack.

Several times during the race, Clarke put on a burst of speed to distance himself from the field, but each time, Mills caught up to him, sometimes taking the lead. Gradually, other runners fell back and out of the race. Only Clarke, Gammoudi, and Mills stayed in front.

At the beginning of the race's final lap, each runner prepared to make his move to take the lead. Clarke moved first, sidestepping another runner on the track, and bumping into Mills in the process. Seeing the collision, Gammoudi surged forward between the two, brushing against both runners, and taking the lead.

Clarke regained stride and closed on Gammoudi, but it was Mills who had the most power left in his sprint. Just a few meters from the finish line, Mills took the lead, breaking the tape just four-tenths of a second in front of second-place Gammoudi, an unbelievably close finish for a 10,000-meter race. Even more unbelievable was Mills' Olympic record time of 28:24.4 seconds—an astonishing 45.6 seconds faster than he had ever run before in this event.

Mills came into the Olympics as an unknown athlete, but he left them an American hero. Nineteen years after he took the gold medal, the movie *Running Brave* was released, chronicling his life and inspirational Olympic achievement.

*Billy Mills was not expected to place in the 10,000 meters. Still, he beat the world record holder and his personal best time to win the gold.*

"Havlicek stole the ball! It's all over! Johnny Havlicek stole the ball!"

Johnny Most

# Havlicek Steal Clinches Celtics Victory

The Boston Celtics of the 1950s and 1960s dominated basketball longer than any other team ever has. From 1957 through 1969, the Celtics won eleven NBA championships in thirteen seasons, including a run of eight titles in a row.

Celtics coach Red Auerbach assembled a team that won more than 70 percent of its games from '57 to '69. With stars Bob Cousy, Bill Russell, and K.C. Jones, the Celtics were nearly unbeatable. They won their first NBA title in 1957, lost to the St. Louis Hawks in 1958, and then began their streak of eight straight titles in 1959.

In 1962, the Celtics drafted John Havlicek, whose role as the Celtics' "sixth man" repeatedly gave the team an injection of energy that carried them to victory. But if there is one moment that came to typify Havlicek's career, it was his steal in the closing seconds of the 1965 Eastern Division Finals. That play also resulted in what is probably basketball's most famous radio call.

The 1965 Eastern Division Finals pitted familiar teams against each other—the Celtics against the Philadelphia 76ers and their all-star center Wilt Chamberlain. In the seventh and deciding game in the series, the Celtics had a 110 to 109 lead with five seconds left. The 76ers had the ball. If they could inbound and score, they would win the series and end the Celtics' championship streak.

Philadelphia's guard Hal Greer was set to inbound the ball. K.C. Jones stood in his way, guarding the inbound pass. Greer looked first to Chamberlain, but Russell guarded him, so Greer looked next to forward Chet Walker. Seeing what was developing, Havlicek hung back for a split second to give Greer the impression that Walker was open. Just as Greer started to release the ball, Havlicek rushed toward Walker and swatted the ball to the floor. Celtics teammate Sam Jones recovered it and ran down the court. Time was up and the Celtics had won by just one point.

Broadcasting the game, Celtics announcer Johnny Most excitedly made the now famous call: "Greer is putting the ball into play....Havlicek steals it. Over to Sam Jones. Havlicek stole the ball! It's all over! Johnny Havlicek stole the ball!" Celtics faithful rushed the floor to celebrate, lifting Havlicek on their shoulders. In their jubilance, they managed to actually tear his jersey off him.

The Celtics went on to beat the Los Angeles Lakers in the finals for their seventh straight NBA title.

*(clockwise from left) Havlicek tips the ball from the hands of Chet Walker.* ■ *Havlicek celebrates on the shoulders of fans and teammates.* ■ *Celtics coach Arnold "Red" Auerbach and his trademark victory cigar.*

"I didn't figure all those people up there in the stands could take the cold for an overtime game."

Vince Lombardi

# Green Bay Packers Win "Ice Bowl"

Vince Lombardi was never much of a gambler. The legendary football coach of the Green Bay Packers won by not taking a lot of chances. But, on one of the few occasions when Lombardi chose to gamble, it paid off with the most memorable win in his career, a championship game remembered by its climate-inspired title, "The Ice Bowl."

It was December 31, 1967, and not surprisingly, the mercury was hovering well below zero in Green Bay. The constant 15-m.p.h. wind whipping through Lambeau Field drove the windchill factor down even further to a numbing 46 degrees Fahrenheit below zero. The playing field was frozen. Adapting a line from Dickens, Packers' Hall of Fame linebacker Ray Nitschke later declared, "It was the worst day for football, and it was also the best day for football." The NFL championship was on the line and, despite the brutal environment, the Dallas Cowboys had come to claim it.

The Packers were used to playing in the harsh conditions. In the game's first quarter, Green Bay quarterback Bart Starr tossed two touchdown passes to Boyd Dowler to give the Packers a confident 14 to 0 lead and it looked like they were on their way to a third straight NFL title. In their previous NFL title game match-up, Dallas had lost to Green Bay 34 to 27. But there were those who believed the Packers were an aging team of veterans ripe for the taking by the younger Cowboys.

Ignoring the Packer lead and the intense cold, the Cowboys started to battle their way back. In the second quarter, Cowboys defensive end George Andrie scooped up a Starr fumble and ran it in for a touchdown. And just before the end of the first half, Packers safety Willie Wood fumbled a punt, setting up a twenty-yard Danny Villanueva field goal to make it 14 to 10. The Cowboys were back in the game and had gained the momentum.

The second half found the Cowboys moving the ball. They took the lead on the first play of the fourth quarter on a fifty-one-yard halfback option pass from Dan Reeves to Lance Rentzel. The score stood at 17 to 14 with the Cowboys in the lead.

*(left to right) Green Bay quarterback Bart Starr (15) makes the winning touchdown for a 21 to 17 victory over the Cowboys.* ■ *Vince Lombardi*

*(above) A sell-out crowd of over fifty thousand braves the sub-zero weather of the Ice Bowl.*

*(opposite page, top to bottom) Packers running back Donny Anderson drives through the Dallas defense. ■ Cowboys quarterback Don Meredith's fumble is recovered by defensive back Herb Adderly during the third quarter of play.*

Down by three points with under five minutes to play, the Packers were sixty-eight yards away from the end zone. Considering the Packers offense hadn't done much since early in the game, an attempt to move into range of a game-tying field goal seemed the likely strategy. Lombardi sent his offense onto the field with Starr and running back Chuck Mercein front and center. Mercein made crucial plays to keep the drive alive, including a nineteen-yard reception from Starr and an eighteen-yard run to the three-yard line. The Packers then ran Donny Anderson twice to get within the one-yard line. They called their final time-out with sixteen seconds left.

Lombardi had a choice to make. He could go for the game-tying field goal and force overtime,

which would have been the conservative option. Or, he could go for the touchdown. But if the Packers were stopped short and stayed in bounds, the clock would run out before Green Bay got another chance.

Lombardi went for the gamble and called for Starr to run the quarterback sneak. Packers right guard Jerry Kramer stood ready, securing his footing on the frozen turf. He was facing Cowboys defensive tackle Jethro Pugh, and on the snap of the ball, Kramer pushed Pugh, whose feet slipped out from underneath him, into the end zone. Starr simply followed in Kramer's wake for the winning touchdown. Lombardi's gamble paid off. The Packers beat the Cowboys 21 to 17 to win their third straight NFL title. "I didn't figure all those people

up there in the stands could take the cold for an overtime game," Lombardi said. "You can't say I'm always without compassion."

Two weeks later, by a score of 33 to 14 over the AFL's Oakland Raiders, Green Bay won Super Bowl II. It would be Lombardi's last game as head coach of the Packers. After five NFL titles and two Super Bowl victories, the mighty Lombardi–Packers dynasty was over. Lombardi coached one more season in the NFL with the Washington Redskins before he died of cancer in 1970. In honor of his contribution to professional football, the Vincent Lombardi Trophy is awarded to Super Bowl championship teams.

"An incredible twenty-nine feet, two and a half inches!"

# Bob Beamon Soars
# to Long Jump Record

At the 1968 Olympic Games, Bob Beamon became the one human on earth who could fly. In the light air of 7,349-foot-high Mexico City, Beamon flew, horizontally, under his own power, longer than any other human in history. And for more than two decades, he held the record as the longest-flying human on the planet.

Though he was expected to do well in the long jump at the 1968 Mexico City Olympics, twenty-two-year-old Beamon barely made the finals. He fouled on his first two qualifying attempts when his toes reached past the front edge of the board from which the jumpers take off. Before his last attempt, teammate Ralph Boston told him to relax, and if he had to, take off from several inches behind the board. The advice worked and Beamon squeaked into the final round.

The next day, in the first round of the finals, Beamon was the fourth jumper. The three competitors ahead of him had fouled. There was a tailwind of 2.0 meters per second, right at the top of the accepted limit. Loose and relaxed, he sprinted down the approach track, gathering speed. Beamon hit the board and leapt, using a personal jumping style he had developed in which his arms and legs "walked" through the air. Mid-flight, six feet in the air, he tucked his knees to his chest. He landed on both feet and rolled forward, nearly at the end of the sand-filled long jump pit.

Olympic officials converged on the pit with their tape measure and carefully checked the distance of the jump. It was several minutes before the results were announced in the stadium, and even longer before the ABC television network was able to report it to those watching. Although the jump aired live, the audio feed was down. An hour later, the audio was restored and the jump was re-broadcast, this time with commentary. The jump had been an unbelievable 8.9 meters— 29 feet 2½ inches. Beamon had smashed the old world record by nearly two feet. When he realized how far he had jumped, he fell to his knees, both in shock and happiness.

Though Beamon never again equaled his record-shattering jump, its sheer magnitude kept him the world's longest-flying man for the next twenty-three years. Indeed, it took another twelve years before any competitor even passed the 28-foot mark. Beamon's record held until 1991, when American Mike Powell bested it by 2 inches at the World Track and Field Championships in Tokyo, Japan.

*Bob Beamon uses his arms and legs to "walk" though the air, and lands near the end of the pit. He broke the world record by almost two feet.*

> "We're gonna win the game. I guarantee it."
>
> Joe Namath

# Joe Namath and Underdog Jets Win Super Bowl III

On January 12, 1969, the NFL was dragged into a new era, not by consensus, but by a cocky, talented, gimpy-kneed quarterback and his team of underdogs. Super Bowl III was the Generation Gap on a football field. On one side of the ball was Johnny Unitas, the Baltimore Colts legendary quarterback—a player nearing the end of his career with his 1950s-style crewcut and business-like professional demeanor. On the other side was New York Jets quarterback "Broadway" Joe Namath with his long hair, sideburns, and outspoken ways.

The game represented more than a cross-cultural challenge; it also symbolized the rivalry between the established National Football League and the upstart American Football League, in only its ninth season. In the first two interleague championships, the NFL's Green Bay Packers had demolished the AFL's Kansas City Chiefs and Oakland Raiders. And there was every indication the third showdown would be no different. The Jets went into the game underdogs against a team that had lost only one game all season.

Three days before the Super Bowl, at a pregame function, the rivalry intensified. During a dinner at the Miami Touchdown Club, Namath, while delivering a speech, responded to a Baltimore heckler by "guaranteeing" a Jets victory. His bold remarks became the cornerstone of Super Bowl coverage in the days leading up to the game.

The media reacted harshly, portraying the young player as nervy, rude, and disrespectful. But for all the criticism, the fans loved it. Football was becoming more than just a game, it was becoming entertainment. On game day, fans packed Miami's Orange Bowl. The game even drew attendance from celebrities such as then soon-to-be president and vice president, Richard Nixon and Spiro Agnew; comedian Jackie Gleason; and astronaut Jim Lovell.

As the game began, those expecting an all-out aerial attack by the Jets—including Colts coach Don Shula—were surprised. He'd primed his team to defend a passing game. But Namath instead deployed an offense of balanced passing and running, keeping the Colts defense from establishing a rhythm.

Reserve quarterback Earl Morrall started the game for the Colts because Unitas was still recovering from a muscle tear in his right elbow. Neither team scored in the first quarter.

The Jets had the ball at the start of the second quarter and Namath engineered a masterful eighty-yard drive. Four consecutive rushes by Matt Snell

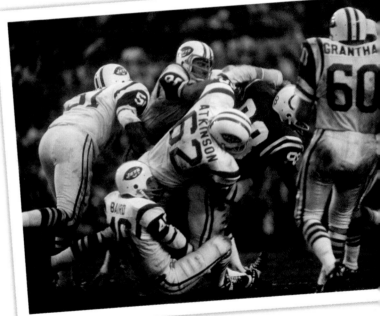

*(left to right) Joe Namath guaranteed a Super Bowl victory and then delivered, leading his team to a 16 to 7 final score.* ■ *Jets defenders swarm to stop Colts tight end John Mackey.*

*(left to right) Baltimore's Johnny Unitas' injuries prevented him from helping his team contend with the Jets. ■ Joe Namath ■ Jets end Matt Snell grabs a pass from Namath for thirty-nine yards in the third quarter.*

got the Jets to midfield. Then Namath passed short to fullback Bill Mathis and the Jets were in Colts territory for the first time. Two throws to George Sauer, a run by Emerson Boozer, and a completion to Snell, and the Jets were inside the ten-yard line. Snell then bulled his way into the end zone and the Jets had the first score. With the extra point, it was 7 to 0 New York.

The Colts came roaring back on their next possession. Their big runner, Tom Matte, galloped for fifty-eight yards, all the way to the Jets sixteen-yard line. Earl Morrall went to the air, only to be intercepted for the second time that day. At the end of the half, Baltimore had one more shot at the end zone. With time running out, Shula called a trick play. Morrall handed off to Matte, and Matte, in turn, lateraled the ball back to Morrall. Morrall threw the ball long but it was picked off again.

(top to bottom) New York's Jim Turner kicks the extra point after a second-quarter touchdown. ■ Joe Namath's passing backed up his bold victory guarantee. ■ Johnny Unitas tries to mount a comeback late in the game.

After halftime, the Colts came out ready to run over the upstart Jets. But it was not to be. On the first play from scrimmage of the second half, the Colts fumbled the ball. Five plays later, the Jets' Jim Turner kicked a field goal and the underdogs were up 10 to 0. As Johnny Unitas began warming up on the sideline, the Colts again failed to score, and gave the ball back to the Jets. Turner booted another field goal and it was 13 to 0 Jets.

Finally, in came Johnny Unitas, but the three-time MVP and future Hall of Famer's arm wasn't completely healed and it showed. Only two of his passes were over twenty yards and both were incomplete. The Jets would score another field goal, the Colts would score a touchdown late in the game, and that would be it. The New York Jets had beaten the mighty Baltimore Colts 16 to 7. It was the first of two Super Bowl victories for the AFL before the two leagues merged, with the former AFL teams becoming part of the NFL's American Football Conference.

In spite of his reputation as a flashy passer, Namath had run his team like a seasoned professional—and he'd made good on his bold guarantee. He never returned to the Super Bowl—but sometimes, if you do it right, once is enough.

"Met fans are pouring on the field—trying to steal home plate, trying to steal the rubber on the mound!"

Lindsey Nelson

# Miracle Mets Win World Series

How can a baseball team that had finished no higher than ninth place since their inaugural year in 1962 win the World Series? If there is an explanation for the miracle of the Mets, it might lie with Hall of Fame pitcher Tom Seaver. Seaver joined the Mets in 1967, won sixteen games, and was named National League Rookie of the Year. Two years later, he had become the team's leader. His amazing 25-7 record was one of the reasons the Mets made it to the playoffs, but it wasn't his only contribution. He was a locker room leader—a winner who expected his teammates to take victory as seriously as he did.

The Mets had struggled their first seven seasons, ending at a total of 288½ games out of first place. But in 1969, the "lovable losers" won thirty-eight of their last forty-nine games, finishing the season with one hundred victories and taking the Eastern Division title. The Mets faced the Atlanta Braves in the National League playoffs and rolled over them, winning three straight games. The Mets won the National League pennant, Seaver had secured his first Cy Young Award, and the team captured the hearts of New York fans.

What stood between the Mets and the championship were the Baltimore Orioles—a team with an awesome arsenal of pitchers and future Hall of Famers like Brooks Robinson and Frank Robinson. When the first game started at Baltimore's Memorial Stadium, it looked like the hapless Mets of old had returned. Even Seaver took his lumps. On his second pitch of the game, Orioles left fielder Don Buford blasted a home run over the fence. Baltimore scored three more runs off of Seaver in the fourth inning for a 4 to 0 lead.

Baltimore, behind the stellar pitching of Mike Cuellar, won the game 4 to 1. Still in Baltimore for game two, the Mets and their pitcher, Jerry Koosman, faced Orioles ace Dave McNally, who had pitched shutouts in his two previous postseason appearances.

Mets first baseman Donn Clendenon homered in the fourth inning, putting the Mets up 1 to 0. In the seventh, Baltimore came back to tie the score, but New York moved ahead for good in the ninth with a small miracle: three consecutive two-out singles that scored a run. In the bottom of the ninth, Baltimore stranded runners on first and second and the Mets won their first World Series game. The series was tied at 1 to 1.

The first World Series game in Shea Stadium was the second win for the Mets. The highlights included two amazing catches by Mets center fielder Tommie

*(left to right) New York Mets catcher Jerry Grote hugs pitcher Jerry Koosman as teammate Ed Charles runs to join the celebration. ▪ Mets pitcher Tom Seaver*

Agee, and reliever Nolan Ryan striking out the Orioles' Paul Blair with the bases loaded in the ninth to earn a save and a 5 to 0 victory.

Game four was not one for the weak of heart. Seaver was on the mound, seeking to avenge his game one loss. The Mets grabbed a 1 to 0 lead early, and Seaver pitched a brilliant game. Then, in the top of the ninth, Baltimore tied the score on a sacrifice fly. The Mets failed to score in the bottom of the ninth, and the game went into extra innings. In the bottom of the tenth inning, the Orioles made a fatal mistake. New York's J.C. Martin bunted, and was hit by the ball as it was thrown to first. The ball bounced into the outfield, allowing Rod Gaspar to score all the way from second base. The Mets went up 3 games to 1.

Game five of the best-of-seven series was again in Shea Stadium where the pitchers from game two, Koosman and McNally, faced off once again. McNally himself opened the scoring in the third inning by hitting a two-run homer. Baltimore's Frank Robinson added to the damage with a solo home run of his own, pushing the score to 3 to 0 in Baltimore's favor.

In the sixth inning, the Mets' Cleon Jones claimed he was hit in the foot by a McNally pitch. The umpire initially denied his claim, but then Mets manager

*(top to bottom) New York first baseman Donn Clendenon homers in the fifth and final game of the World Series.*
■ *Center fielder Tommie Agee makes a diving catch with the bases loaded in the seventh inning of game three.*

Gil Hodges showed the umpire the baseball. On it was a smudge of black shoe polish. The umpire waved Jones to first base. The very next batter, Donn Clendenon, homered and put the Mets on the scoreboard. The score was 3 to 2.

In the seventh inning, Mets infielder Al Weis, a player who had hit a mere five home runs in his career in the majors, stepped to the plate and knocked one over the left field fence, tying the score. In the bottom of the eighth, back-to-back doubles put the Mets up by one run. Later in the inning, Boog Powell, the huge Baltimore first baseman, committed an error, allowing the Mets' Ron Swoboda to score from second. Jerry Koosman held the Orioles scoreless in the ninth and the miracle was complete. The record crowd of 57,397 erupted.

Fans poured onto the field, crazed, delirious, exuberant, dazed, happy. In a celebratory display, fans stole home plate and the pitcher's rubber, then covered the outfield walls with chalked graffiti. Their celebration then spilled onto the streets of New York. After all, they'd witnessed a miracle—the Mets had won the World Series!

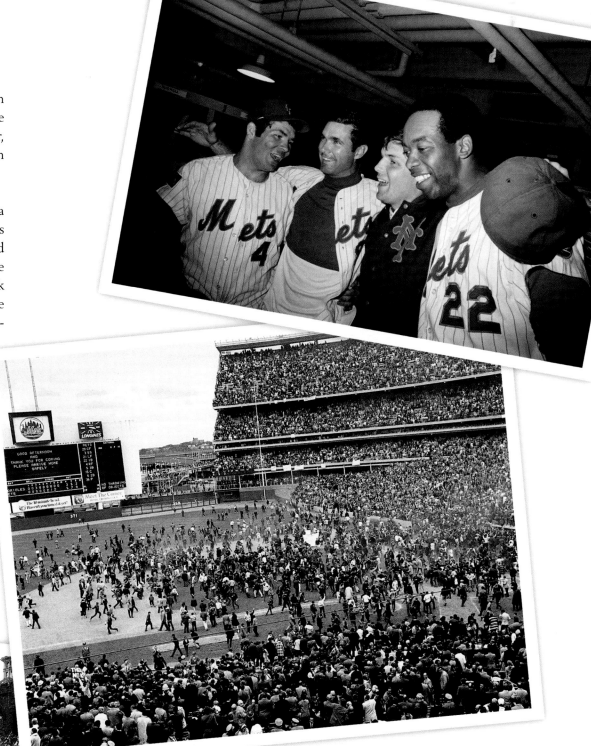

*(top to bottom) Ron Swoboda, J.C. Martin, Tom Seaver, and Donn Clendenon celebrate in the locker room after the game. ■ Fans storm the field at Shea Stadium just seconds after the World Series win. ■ The day after New York's victory, businesspeople hustle through the aftermath of the celebration.*

"Here comes Willis!
The crowd is going wild!"

Marv Albert

# Willis Reed Leads Knicks to Victory

Entering the 1969-70 regular season, the New York Knicks had never won an NBA title, but they had assembled a solid team with Walt Frazier, Bill Bradley, Dave DeBusschere, and Willis Reed. Frazier was the playmaker and top defensive guard. Bradley was the outside shooter. DeBusschere was a jump shooter and tough defensive forward. And Reed, the undersized center, scored, rebounded, played defense, and did whatever it took to win.

With this cast of players, and coach Red Holzman, the Knicks won sixty of eighty-two regular season games. In the playoffs, they beat the Baltimore Bullets and the Milwaukee Bucks. The Knicks advanced to the NBA championship series against the Los Angeles Lakers, a team with its own stars— Elgin Baylor, Wilt Chamberlain, and Jerry West.

Reed dominated game one, scoring thirty-seven points and leading the Knicks to a 124 to 112 victory. By game five, the series was tied at 2-2. But in game five, Reed tore a muscle in his right thigh. It forced him from the game, which the Knicks won 107 to 100. But with Reed out for game six, the Knicks had no one to contest the 7-foot 1-inch Chamberlain, who scored forty-five points and grabbed twenty-seven rebounds to give the Lakers a victory. The series went to a decisive game seven.

The Knicks faced the Lakers in the final, winner-take-all game on May 8, 1970, in New York. With

Reed out of the game, the Lakers were favored to win. Reed's thigh injury had not responded to treatment and still badly hurt him. The Knicks left the locker room not knowing if Reed would be able to play. Then, minutes before tip-off, Reed hobbled onto the court in obvious pain. New York fans responded with an ovation that began to return confidence to the entire team.

George Kalinsky, the official photographer for Madison Square Garden, recalled an "electricity in the crowd that I had never felt in the Garden before."

Seconds after the opening tip, Reed scored the game's first basket. On the Knicks' next trip down the floor, he scored again, and the crowd wildly cheered his courageous effort.

Reed didn't score the rest of the game, but continued playing on a near-useless leg, leaving the game only when the Knicks had a sizable, twenty-four-point lead. He played solid defense against Chamberlain, limiting the Lakers' ability to score from inside. More importantly, he inspired his team and energized the crowd. The Knicks won the game 113 to 99 to capture their first NBA championship.

*(clockwise from left) An injured Reed arrives for game seven.* ■ *Reed sustains an injury in game five.* ■ *Reed snares a rebound in front of Chamberlain.*

"He's won everything
he had hoped to win!"
Keith Jackson

# Mark Spitz Wins Record Seven Gold Medals

Mark Spitz was raised to be a swimmer and groomed to be a champion. As a competitive swimmer in his youth, he established age-specific world record times and brought home national and international championships. He had attitude, discipline, determination, and a long powerful body that glided through the water.

By the age of eighteen, Spitz was ready for his first Olympics, the 1968 Mexico City Games. Although he predicted he would win six gold medals at Mexico City, he fell short, winning two team golds for relay, a silver in the 100-meter butterfly, and a bronze in the 100-meter freestyle. It was a good Olympics for most, but not good enough for Spitz.

He returned home to attend Indiana University, where he won the 1971 Sullivan Award as the nation's top amateur athlete. He was now ready for the 1972 Olympic Games in Munich, West Germany. During an eight-day span, Spitz dominated the Olympics like no other athlete before or since.

Spitz was the favorite in his first race, the 200-meter butterfly, and won the gold in a world record time of 2:00.7. Later that same day, he anchored the American 400-meter freestyle relay team to another world record of 3:26.42, and a gold medal.

The next day, Spitz came from behind to win the 200-meter freestyle. It was another gold medal and another world record time of 1:52.78. After one day of rest, Spitz competed again in the 100-meter butterfly and on the 800-meter freestyle relay team. The results continued the pattern he was establishing: two more gold medals and two more world records, for a total of five each in the Games.

On September 3, Spitz faced the most serious challenge to his gold medal streak in the 100-meter freestyle, a sprint race where one mistake could mean the difference between gold and silver. American Jerry Heidenreich was given a good chance to win, but Spitz took the lead from the start and never lost it. It was another gold medal and another world record finish of 51.22 seconds.

The seventh gold medal for Spitz was almost a foregone conclusion as he swam the butterfly leg on the victorious American 400-meter medley relay team. ABC Television, with Keith Jackson anchoring, broadcast the historic moment back to the U.S. In his inimitable staccato delivery, Jackson gave voice to the excitement of the moment: "And there is Mark Spitz churning furiously through the water, heading for the final twenty-five meters." All the while his volume increased as he tried to keep up with the cheering of the crowd, which grew louder with the completion of each leg of the race.

*(left to right) Mark Spitz* ■ *Mark Spitz in 1968. He predicted he would win six gold medals in the '68 Olympics. He won only two.*

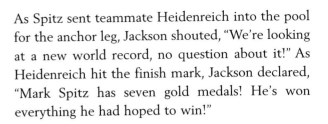

As Spitz sent teammate Heidenreich into the pool for the anchor leg, Jackson shouted, "We're looking at a new world record, no question about it!" As Heidenreich hit the finish mark, Jackson declared, "Mark Spitz has seven gold medals! He's won everything he had hoped to win!"

Hours after Spitz won his final gold medal, the Munich games were rocked by Palestinian terrorists who stormed the Olympic Village apartments housing the Israeli Olympic team. In all, eleven members of the Israeli contingent were killed. The peaceful aims of the Olympic ideal were crushed. Spitz, fearful for his own safety because of his popularity and Jewish descent, left the Olympics before the closing ceremonies.

*(top to bottom) Spitz trains for the 100-meter butterfly before the '72 Olympics.* ■ *Soviet swimmer Vladimir Bure celebrates his third-place finish as Spitz looks for his winning time in the 100-meter freestyle.* ■ *Spitz shows off five of his seven gold medals.*

Mark Spitz returned to America as a hero and one of history's greatest Olympic athletes. His nine Olympic gold medals tie him for the most ever with American sprinter Carl Lewis, Soviet gymnast Larissa Latynina, and Finnish long-distance runner Paavo Nurmi. His eleven total Olympic medals tie him with swimmer Matt Biondi and shooter Carl Osburn as the all-time winningest American athletes.

But no athlete besides Mark Spitz ever won seven gold medals and set seven world records during just one Olympics, and no one ever dominated a sport like Spitz dominated swimming at the 1972 Olympic Games.

*(top to bottom) Spitz celebrates with teammates after his seventh gold medal. The relay team broke the world record for the 400-meter medley. ■ Spitz displays the victory symbol after winning his fourth medal in the 200-meter butterfly.*

"I don't think there's a basketball game that has me so totally confused as the ending to this one."

Chris Schenkel

# Olympic Basketball Team Upset by Soviets

The Cold War met the basketball court on September 10, 1972, when Team USA, undefeated in Olympic play since the game's introduction in 1936, met a powerful Soviet team. Those looking to the game for a peaceful athletic contest between two countries at odds, however, would only find conflict and disappointment.

Though heavily favored, the U.S. worked for much of the game to catch up to their competitors. They narrowed a five-point deficit at the half to just one point with thirty seconds left in the game. With six seconds on the clock, future NBA player and coach Doug Collins intercepted a Soviet pass and drove hard to the basket. As he attempted to score, he was smashed to the ground by a Soviet player. The foul nearly rendered him unconscious.

After a frightening moment for the American team, Collins was able to rise to his feet. He then made both foul shots to put his team in the lead 50 to 49. Three seconds remained on the clock.

Immediately after Collins' second free-throw shot, the Soviet team called for a time-out. Their request was not granted because international rules prohibited time-outs directly after free throws. The officials ordered the Soviets to first inbound the ball.

But instead of inbounding and then calling for a time-out, the Soviet team threw the ball in and

stormed onto the court in protest of the referee's decision. Though the crowd, and the announcers, thought that time had run out, signifying a U.S. victory, an official stopped the clock at one second to clear the court.

"Now we're being told the scoreboard is not correct," play-by-play announcer Frank Gifford told viewers watching the game on ABC Television. "Well," he said, "confusion reigns."

Once order resumed, the Soviets threw in a second inbound pass, but failed to deliver the winning basket as the clock ran to zero.

The U.S. team again started celebrating their eighth consecutive Olympic gold medal. Fans in the stands were still on their feet cheering when R. William Jones, the secretary general for the International Amateur Basketball Federation (FIBA), approached the referees' table. Though Jones had no authority over any Olympic games, he managed to overrule the officials, restore three seconds to the game, and grant the Soviets their previously denied time-out.

*(left to right) Team USA's Kevin Joyce fights for possession of the ball. ■ U.S. and Soviet players race for a loose ball.*

The Soviets again had possession out-of-bounds, and American forward Tom McMillen stood ready. McMillen's aggressive guarding of inbound passer Ivan Edeshko, however, attracted the attention of Brazilian referee Renato Righetto. Though no rule supported his demand, Righetto ordered McMillen to back away from the Russian. With little defense against him, Edeshko was able to throw the ball down the court into the hands of teammate Aleksander Belov.

Belov grabbed the ball, leapt over heavy U.S. defense, and threw the ball through the hoop. "The time is over!" proclaimed Gifford. In a stunning and controversial upset, the Soviet Union had defeated the United States 51 to 50.

*(top to bottom) U.S. player Ed Ratleff (15) contests a shot by Soviet opponent Alshan Sharmukhamedov (7). ■ Aleksander Belov scores the game-winning basket after grabbing a floor-length pass from Ivan Edeshko. ■ U.S. coach Hank Iba, wearing the dark suit, attempts to explain his team's case to referees following the loss to the Soviet Union. Iba returned to the locker room to find he had been pickpocketed during the dispute.*

(top to bottom) The Soviet team celebrates their controversial win. ■ Soviet player Ivan Edeshko raises his arms in victory.

The Soviet players erupted on the court, falling over one another in the excitement of the moment. The stunned U.S. team, however, exited the arena after failing to persuade officials to reverse the game's ending.

"You know, we've covered a lot of basketball games over the years for ABC, and I don't think there's a basketball game that has me so totally confused as the ending to this one," anchorman Chris Schenkel confessed to viewers.

The American team quickly filed an appeal with FIBA, but was denied in a 3 to 2 decision. Every member of the U.S. Olympic basketball team boycotted the awards ceremony and refused the silver medal. The medals remain in a vault in Switzerland, and, according to a ruling by the International Olympic Committee, will be claimed only if the 1972 team unanimously agrees to accept them.

In subsequent Olympic years, many of the American players turned down opportunities of a silver medal ceremony. Though decades passed, the pain of their loss to the Soviets did not. Collins later admitted, "Nothing comes close to the feeling of a twenty-one-year-old kid playing for his country and winning the gold, nothing comes close to the feeling I should've had if they hadn't taken it away from me."

"Franco Harris pulled in the football—I don't even know where it came from!"

Jack Fleming

# "The Immaculate Reception": Steelers vs. Raiders

The Pittsburgh Steelers' dominance over professional football in the 1970s began on December 23, 1972, at Pittsburgh's Three Rivers Stadium. The Central Division champions hosted the Western Division champion Oakland Raiders in the AFC Divisional playoff game.

The game was a defensive struggle, but a late touchdown by Raiders quarterback Ken Stabler put his team in the lead, 7 to 6. After the ensuing kickoff, the Steelers took over at their own twenty-yard line with just 1:13 left in the game. Steelers quarterback Terry Bradshaw moved the ball forward on two completed passes, but with twenty-two seconds left, he faced fourth down and ten yards to go from their own forty-yard line, well beyond field goal range.

Bradshaw called a play with receiver Barry Pearson as his first passing option, and running back John "Frenchy" Fuqua as the second. From the beginning, everything on the play went wrong. The Raiders' defensive line flushed Bradshaw from the pocket. Running back Franco Harris saw Bradshaw in trouble and left the backfield to position himself as a potential receiver.

Bradshaw never saw Pearson, but did spot Fuqua across the middle about twenty yards downfield and fired the ball to him. The ball arrived to Fuqua at the same time Raiders defensive back Jack

Tatum hit Fuqua from behind. It went flying backward about fifteen yards as Fuqua fell to the ground.

The ball ricocheted toward Harris, who caught the ball off his shoe tops and raced downfield, evading one last Raiders defender en route to the end zone for an incredible sixty-yard touchdown. Fans and players stormed the field, despite the fifteen seconds still on the clock and a delayed ruling as to the validity of the final run.

The Raiders contended that it was an illegal pass and should not have counted because the ball bounced off Fuqua to Harris. The rule at the time was that a pass could not be tipped from one offensive player to another without a defensive player also touching the ball.

But referee Fred Swearingen ruled that the Raiders' Jack Tatum also had touched the ball, making it a legal catch and a touchdown. The Steelers kicked the extra point and won the game 13 to 7. Pittsburgh lost the next week to the Miami Dolphins in the AFC Championship game 21 to 17. But their playoff win against the Raiders, capped off by the "Immaculate Reception," laid the groundwork for the rest of the decade, in which the Steelers would win four Super Bowl titles.

*(clockwise from left) Franco Harris runs to the end zone for the game-winning touchdown.* ■ *Raiders defensive back Jack Tatum hits Frenchy Fuqua, sending the ball flying.* ■ *Harris lunges to catch the ball and manages to keep his balance.*

"He's going to be the Triple Crown winner.... An unbelievable, an amazing performance."

Chick Anderson

# Secretariat Wins Triple Crown

In the spring of 1973, Secretariat set out to win horse racing's Triple Crown, something that had not been done since Citation won the Kentucky Derby, the Preakness, and the Belmont Stakes in 1948. Secretariat didn't just win races, he destroyed the field on numerous occasions. Lucien Laurin trained the three-year-old colt, owned by Penny Tweedy, and with jockey Ron Turcotte, it appeared the horse had a winning advantage.

Though Secretariat was favored to win the Kentucky Derby, there was some doubt about the horse because of a third-place finish in the Wood Memorial two weeks prior. Laurin continued to train Secretariat and felt confident the horse had improved. The training paid off. Secretariat ran the Derby in a record time of 1:59.40 to take the first leg of horse racing's Triple Crown.

The Preakness was next, and once again, Secretariat was the dominant horse. The race began with a slow pace, and Turcotte, knowing Secretariat had the speed to win, didn't push him. Secretariat responded to the jockey's hands-off approach with an easy two and one-half length victory over Sham, the second-place horse.

The final leg of the Triple Crown was the Belmont Stakes in Belmont Park, New York. Secretariat was set to race against only four competitors. On June 9, 1973, nearly seventy thousand race fans at Belmont Park and a nationwide television audience watched Secretariat run to fame.

At one and one-half miles, the Belmont Stakes is the longest of the Triple Crown races. Its length has ruined many a horse's chance at winning the sought-after honor. It was a two-horse race for the first half, as Secretariat battled rival Sham. The early pace was extremely fast and it seemed both horses might burn themselves out.

*(left to right) Turcotte and Secretariat win the Kentucky Derby in record time.* ■ *Turcotte turns to observe the extent of Secretariat's lead in the Belmont Stakes.*

Even before the halfway point, Secretariat and Sham led the rest of the field by ten lengths. As they headed into the turn at the end of the backstretch, Secretariat started to pull away from Sham, and the race between the two became a solo sprint. "He is moving like a tremendous machine! Secretariat by twelve!" track announcer Chick Anderson yelled. The crowd watched in amazement as Secretariat's lead increased from twelve lengths, to fourteen on the final turn, to eighteen lengths, then twenty-two.

Anderson continued to call the race, "He is going to be the Triple Crown winner....He hits the finish twenty-five lengths in front!" It was as if the other horses were walking while Secretariat galloped down the home stretch. The lead was so large, the CBS camera covering the stretch run had difficulty showing Secretariat and second-place Twice a Prince in the same shot.

*(left to right) Although more than one unofficial timer clocked Secretariat's Preakness time as beating the record of 1:54, the official time stood at 1:54.4.*
■ *Secretariat in the Kentucky Derby*
■ *Turcotte and Secretariat race in the final leg of the Triple Crown.*

Secretariat crossed the finish line an amazing thirty-one lengths ahead of Twice a Prince, breaking the Belmont Stakes' track record by 2.6 seconds and finishing with a time of 2:24.

"I finally had to turn to see where the other horses were," jockey Turcotte later recalled.

Secretariat raced six more times after winning the Triple Crown, winning four races and finishing second twice. In twenty-one career starts, Secretariat won sixteen races. His racing career was short, and though eight before him had won the Triple Crown, no horse ever dominated a race like Secretariat did in the 1973 Belmont Stakes.

Secretariat ran and won his final race in October 1973. He was later sold to a breeding syndicate for $6.08 million, siring future champions Risen Star (1988 Preakness and Belmont winner) and 1986 Horse of the Year, Lady's Secret.

*(top to bottom) Turcotte poses with Secretariat after their victory in the Kentucky Derby.* ■ *Secretariat won the Preakness by two and one-half lengths.*

"It is over!…
The long-
awaited match,
hustled and
promoted
ceaselessly and
shrewdly by
Bobby Riggs."
Howard Cosell

# Billie Jean King Wins "Battle of the Sexes"

Though Billie Jean King first entered Centre Court at Wimbledon eighty-two years after women began winning championships there, women athletes still had to fight for equal respect and consideration. When King won her first Wimbledon singles title in 1966, the women's first prize was a gift certificate for tennis clothing. When King won her third singles title in 1968, her winnings were only slightly more than one-third that of her male counterpart, Rod Laver.

In 1970, still angered by the inequality between male and female tennis players' earnings, King spearheaded the successful Virginia Slims circuit, a separate tour for female tennis professionals. In her own career, she worked to even the playing field in terms of both gender and salary. By 1971, she became the first female pro tennis player to break the $100,000 earnings mark in a single year.

Having broken a salary barrier, King then worked to strengthen the image of female athletes. She won back-to-back Wimbledon titles in 1972 and 1973, and then accepted a challenge from former tennis star Bobby Riggs that would make her a household name.

In 1973, Bobby Larimore Riggs was fifty-five years old and a retired Wimbledon champion. Thirty-four years before, in 1939, Bobby went to the English tournament virtually unknown and took advantage of his anonymity. He placed a large bet on himself, wagering he'd win the singles, doubles, and mixed doubles competitions. And he did just that. Later that year, he was ranked the No. 1 tennis player in the world.

By 1973 Riggs' career as a pro had been over for more than two decades, but he remained in the game, promoting tennis matches and hustling younger opponents with an array of spins, drop shots, and lobs. A shameless self-promoter, Riggs sought notoriety by challenging the top women's professionals of the day to a match. The first "Battle of the Sexes" was held on

*(clockwise from left) King celebrates her victory in the Battle of the Sexes. ■ King displays her trophies in 1967. By the end of her career, King had won 20 Wimbledon titles in singles, doubles, and mixed doubles events. ■ Bobby Riggs lunges for a ball during a match in New York City in 1940.*

Mother's Day, May 12, 1973, with Riggs using his arsenal of trick shots to beat the top-ranked women's champion, Margaret Court, in straight sets. A twenty-nine-year-old King agreed to play a much older Riggs in a Battle of the Sexes rematch.

Thanks to an unending barrage of publicity, both by the event's promoters and the media, the Battle of the Sexes became one of the most discussed events of the year. Corporate sponsorship poured in—with money and advertising backing both players. The television networks fought each other for broadcast rights, with ABC ultimately out-bidding CBS. They also assigned two of their best play-by-play men, Howard Cosell and Frank Gifford, to call the match.

The contest was held in the Houston Astrodome in front of more than thirty thousand people, with forty million more watching on television, making it the most-watched tennis match in history. Each of the contenders entered the arena on rickshaw-like carts. While a team of chiseled male athletes pulled King into the arena, Riggs was pulled in by a group of female models named "Bobby's Bosom Buddies." The two met and Riggs presented his challenger with a giant-sized lollipop. King gifted Riggs with a baby pig named "Larimore Hustle."

The match began with King clearly the more aggressive and confident competitor. She smashed

*(left to right) King and Riggs promote their upcoming Battle of the Sexes in a news conference. ■ King is carried into the Astrodome.*

shots past Riggs, shots his middle-aged legs just didn't have the speed to reach. Riggs' arsenal of junk shots was useless if he couldn't get to the ball. King won the first set 6-4, and went on to win the second set 6-3. Now in full control of the match, she took the third and final set 6-3, winning the second Battle of the Sexes.

As absurd as this gender challenge might have been, it sent a powerful and positive message to early 1970s society—that women athletes could compete with men. In the end, it became an incredible irony. Bobby Riggs, the "male chauvinist pig" who set out to prove the inferiority of female athletes, was the man many now credit with making women's tennis, and women's athletics as a whole, the force they are today.

*(top to bottom) King demolishes Riggs in three straight sets. ■ King and Riggs, who remained good friends after the match, shake hands after Riggs' defeat.*

**"There's a new home run champion of all time, and it's Henry Aaron."**

Milo Hamilton

# Henry Aaron Breaks Home Run Record

Perhaps because Hank Aaron was a quiet man, or because he lacked the bravado often associated with athletes, Aaron's outstanding athletic abilities didn't thrust him into the spotlight—that is, not until he shattered one of the most hallowed of all baseball records.

Henry Louis Aaron was born in Mobile, Alabama, on February 5, 1934, and by the time he was seventeen years old he had been signed by the Negro League's Indianapolis Clowns. Aaron had great potential at the plate, despite the fact that he batted cross-handed—though he was right-handed, he gripped the bat with his left hand on top instead of his right. Even so, he was an incredible hitter.

Aaron's raw talent was so instantly evident that he didn't complete a full season with the Clowns before the big leagues beckoned. The Milwaukee Braves quickly bought out Aaron's contract, uncrossed his hands, and sent him to their Class A farm team. When the 1954 season started, he was supposed to move up to AAA ball—a promotion, but still not the major leagues. But then fate stepped in. Veteran outfielder Bobby Thomson was injured in spring training. Aaron filled his place the next day in the Braves lineup. In his first preseason at-bat, he hit a home run, sealing his place on the Braves' roster. Aaron stayed with the Braves for the next two decades, moving with the team to Atlanta in 1966.

Aaron's rise to the major leagues taught him not only the skills of upper-level baseball, but the ways of African American ball players. Though great players like Aaron, Jackie Robinson, and Willie Mays possessed more talent than most of their white teammates, America's racial intolerance forced them to lead separate lives off the field. While on the road, African American players had to sleep in segregated hotels, eat in separate restaurants, and endure the scorn of racist fans. Aaron and his fellow major league African Americans endured the injustices with grace and dignity that would slowly help break racial barriers. Rather than lash out, they focused their energies on excelling at the game they loved.

Aaron started to shine in 1955. That season was the first of nineteen years in which he hit twenty or more home runs, the first of thirteen seasons his batting average would top .300, and the first of eleven seasons he'd knock in more than one hundred runs.

After fifteen years in the majors, Aaron was within reach of several high profile major league records. Though he considered retiring during the '69 season, he shelved such thoughts in the hopes of revealing the racism in major league baseball. Perhaps if he broke the records, he could finally get a national audience for his cause.

*(left to right) Hank Aaron holds his 715th home run ball up for the sell-out crowd in Atlanta. ■ Aaron watches the flight of what would become his 715th home run.*

In 1970, he passed three thousand hits, putting him in the rare company of legends like Ty Cobb, Stan Musial, and Honus Wagner. He then took off after Babe Ruth's career home run record. In 1971, at the age of thirty-seven, he hit a career-high forty-seven home runs and batted .327. That earned him a two-year contract that made him the first player to annually earn $200,000. Aaron finished the '72 season just forty-one homers short of the Babe's "unbreakable" record.

But just as certain fans didn't like Roger Maris breaking the Babe's single-season home run record in 1961, vehemence against Aaron raged the closer he got to "lucky" number 714. People sent hate mail and fans booed him at the parks, flinging racial

*(top to bottom) Aaron before a game in May 1959 ■ After twenty years in the majors, Aaron hits his 715th home run and breaks Babe Ruth's record.*

slurs fast and furious. During the 1973 season, he dealt with death threats to himself and to his family, forcing him to employ a bodyguard. Still, by the end of the season he was at 713 home runs—just one short of the record.

The 1974 season started with another controversy. The Braves were to start the year with a three-game stand at Cincinnati, and Braves management announced that Aaron would be held out of the lineup so he could hit the record-breaker at their home field. Commissioner Bowie Kuhn, however, ordered that Aaron play in the first three games. Playing in two of those three games, Aaron managed to tie the record, but not break it.

April 8, 1974, was Hank Aaron Night at Atlanta-Fulton County Stadium, and the crowd didn't have long to wait for the main event. Forty-year-old Hank Aaron, in his 2,967th game in the majors, stepped up to the plate in the third inning against veteran Dodgers pitcher Al Downing. Downing's first pitch was a ball, low. The crowd booed, then hushed as they awaited the next pitch.

It was a fastball, and the waiting was over. More than fifty thousand paying customers in the stadium, and millions viewing on television, watched as

the ball flew over the left field wall and Henry Louis Aaron, a product of the Negro Leagues, did the Babe one better, and victoriously ran the bases and into history.

For more than two minutes, the stadium erupted in a celebration of cheering and fireworks. "There's a new home run champion of all time, and it's Henry Aaron.…Listen to this crowd!" cried play-by-play announcer Milo Hamilton.

Aaron was visibly relieved as he touched down on home plate. There, he was met by his teammates, his father Herbert Sr., and his mother, Estella. Later, reflecting on the difficulties his bid for the record had caused his family and himself, Aaron said, "Thank God it's over."

*(left to right) Fans storm the field before Aaron finishes running the bases.*
*■ Aaron tips his hat to teammates and fans who wait for him at home plate.*
*■ Aaron greets his parents after his record-breaking home run. Later he admitted, "I never knew that my mother could hug so tight."*

### Hank Aaron's Career Statistics

| | |
|---|---|
| Home Runs | 755 |
| Hits | 3,771 |
| RBIs | 2,297 |
| Total Bases | 6,856 |

"I am the King!"

Cassius Clay

# Muhammad Ali:
# Three-Time Heavyweight Champion

Muhammad Ali's superstar skill and powerful personality are all his own, but he owes his start to a concerned policeman and a flamboyant 1950s wrestler.

In 1954, a twelve-year-old Cassius Marcellus Clay Jr. had his bicycle stolen from him. Louisville, Kentucky, policeman Joe Elsby Martin advised him that if he wanted to hold on to his next bike, it would be a good idea if he learned how to box. He took the patrolman's advice and discovered he was a natural.

While Clay was developing his boxing jabs, he was also developing his verbal jabs. He has said he drew inspiration from a professional wrestler named Gorgeous George, a dyed-blonde who infuriated crowds and opponents by preening, pouting, and proclaiming how "pretty" he was.

By the age of eighteen, Clay had compiled a record of 108 wins against eight losses in amateur competition. In 1959, he won the International Golden Gloves heavyweight title, and, a year later, represented the United States at the 1960 Olympics in Rome, Italy, where he won the gold medal in the light heavyweight division. After the Olympics, he returned home and went professional.

Over the next four years, Clay gained a reputation both as a fearsome fighter and a big-time talker, earning himself nicknames like the "Louisville Lip" and "Mighty Mouth." By 1964, he had earned a shot at the heavyweight title, at the time held by powerhouse Sonny Liston, an ex-convict who'd grown up in a house with twenty-five brothers and sisters. Liston was said to have the most vicious stare in professional sports, and he'd won the title two years earlier by knocking out Floyd Patterson in the very first round of the fight.

Clay was a major underdog, a brash boy boxing a street-smart man. But such odds did not stop him from making one of his famous predictions. Boldly breaking sporting etiquette of the time, Clay publicly pronounced that he'd knock Liston out in the eighth round, boasting that he'd "float like a butterfly, sting like a bee."

*(clockwise from left) Only one minute into the first round of their 1965 rematch, Clay knocks out Liston to retain his heavyweight crown. ■ Twelve-year-old Cassius Clay ■ Clay and teammates in the 1960 Rome Olympics*

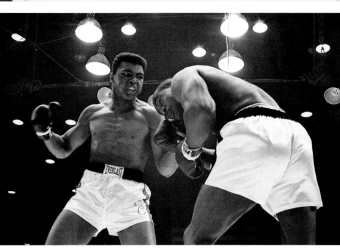

(clockwise from upper left) Following the Liston-Patterson title fight, Clay holds up fingers to indicate he will take Liston's heavyweight title in eight rounds. July 23, 1963 ▪ Ali punches Liston in the fight that would give him his first heavyweight champion title. ▪ Ali has to be restrained after beating Liston in 1964. ▪ Ali taunts Liston to get up in the first round of their rematch. May 1965

Before the fight started, the odds were 8 to 1 in Liston's favor. But Clay's dance and jab were too much for the older Liston. He sat down in his corner after the sixth round and failed to answer the bell at the beginning of the seventh.

Clay was crowned the Heavyweight Champion of the World, and bestowed upon himself the title "The Greatest." Soon after the fight, he proclaimed his allegiance to the Nation of Islam, and changed his name. As Muhammad Ali, he successfully

defended his title, including a 1965 rematch against Liston. Ali won the second bout quickly and easily, knocking the challenger out in the first round. But Ali's reign as champion came to an end early in 1967.

It wasn't another fighter who took the title, it was the United States Draft Board. The war in Vietnam was escalating, and so was the protest movement. Ali received his draft notice and refused induction on religious grounds, claiming conscientious objector status. He was supported by his brethren in the Nation of Islam, but his protest alienated a large portion of the public who supported the war. He was convicted of draft evasion, stripped of his championship, and banned from boxing by the New York State Athletic Commission, with other boxing commissions joining the ban. The heavyweight title was declared vacant.

While Ali fought the government, others fought in the ring, and another Olympic gold medalist, "Smokin'" Joe Frazier, punched his way to the title. Meanwhile, Ali's conviction was on appeal with the U.S. Supreme Court. While awaiting the

Court's decision, Ali continued to fight where he was allowed, scoring a third-round technical knockout against Jerry Quarry and a fifteen-round TKO over Oscar Bonavena. Ali faced Frazier in March 1971 in what was later called "The Fight of the Century." Although Ali received a guaranteed $2.5 million purse, he lost in a fifteen-round decision.

The sting of the crushing loss to Frazier was lessened later that year when the U.S. Supreme Court finally ruled in Ali's favor. He could once again set his sights on the championship belt. In 1974, Ali had regained form, defeating Frazier to earn a shot at the new champion, George Foreman, yet another Olympic gold medal winner. The bout, held in Kinshasa, Zaire, was promoted as "The Rumble in the Jungle."

As was usual with an Ali fight, the buildup was as exciting as the event itself. The match was scheduled for September 25, 1974, but was delayed over a month after Foreman suffered a deep cut over his eye during training. Ali took the opportunity to train, gain local fans, and develop a new ring strategy.

*(upper left) Clay arrives at the U.S. Army Induction Center.* ■ *(at right) Ali and Frazier slug it out during the 1971 "Fight of the Century." Ali lost in a fifteen-round decision.*

The fight finally took place on October 30, 1974, in a rebuilt soccer stadium in front of a sell-out crowd and millions more watching on television. Ali, who'd spent the weeks before the fight predicting he'd dance around Foreman and dazzle him with his footwork, proceeded to unveil what he later called the "rope-a-dope." He hugged the ring ropes and let Foreman pound on him in the early rounds. But later in the fight, Ali's strategy became evident. Foreman got tired, his arms got heavy, and Ali charged in, taking him apart with precise, powerful punching. In the eighth round, "The Rumble in the Jungle" was over. Ali knocked Foreman out to win his second heavyweight championship.

After Ali had defended his title three times in early 1975, he agreed to fight Joe Frazier again. They'd each won one of their two previous fights, and this, the tiebreaker, was held in the stifling heat of Quezon City, Philippines, and was billed as "The Thrilla in Manila." The fight, witnessed by twenty-eight thousand in person and a reported seven hundred million on television, was one of the classic

*(clockwise from upper left) Ali uses his "rope-a-dope" strategy against Foreman.* ■ *Ali celebrates as referee Zack Clayton counts Foreman out in the eighth round. October 30, 1974* ■ *Ali clings to the ropes in "The Rumble in the Jungle."*

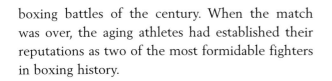

boxing battles of the century. When the match was over, the aging athletes had established their reputations as two of the most formidable fighters in boxing history.

Ali took the early rounds, but in the middle of the fight, Frazier rebounded with an attack to Ali's mid-section. Ali turned the fight around in the 11th, standing toe-to-toe with Frazier and slugging it out. By the 14th round, both veterans were exhausted and Frazier's eyes were swollen nearly shut. When the bell rang to start the 15th and last round, Frazier's corner stopped the fight. By all accounts, it was the most brutal fight in Ali's career.

Muhammad Ali defended his title six more times after defeating Frazier a second time, and finally lost the title in February 1978 to Leon Spinks. But that wasn't the end of Ali. Seven months later, he and Spinks fought again. With Ali winning in fifteen rounds and regaining the heavyweight championship, he became the first boxer in history to win the title three different times.

*(top to bottom) Ali hits Frazier with a hard right during the seventh round of their 1975 rematch. ■ Ali versus Frazier in "The Thrilla in Manila" ■ Ali and Frazier slug it out in Quezon City for what would be called Ali's most brutal fight.*

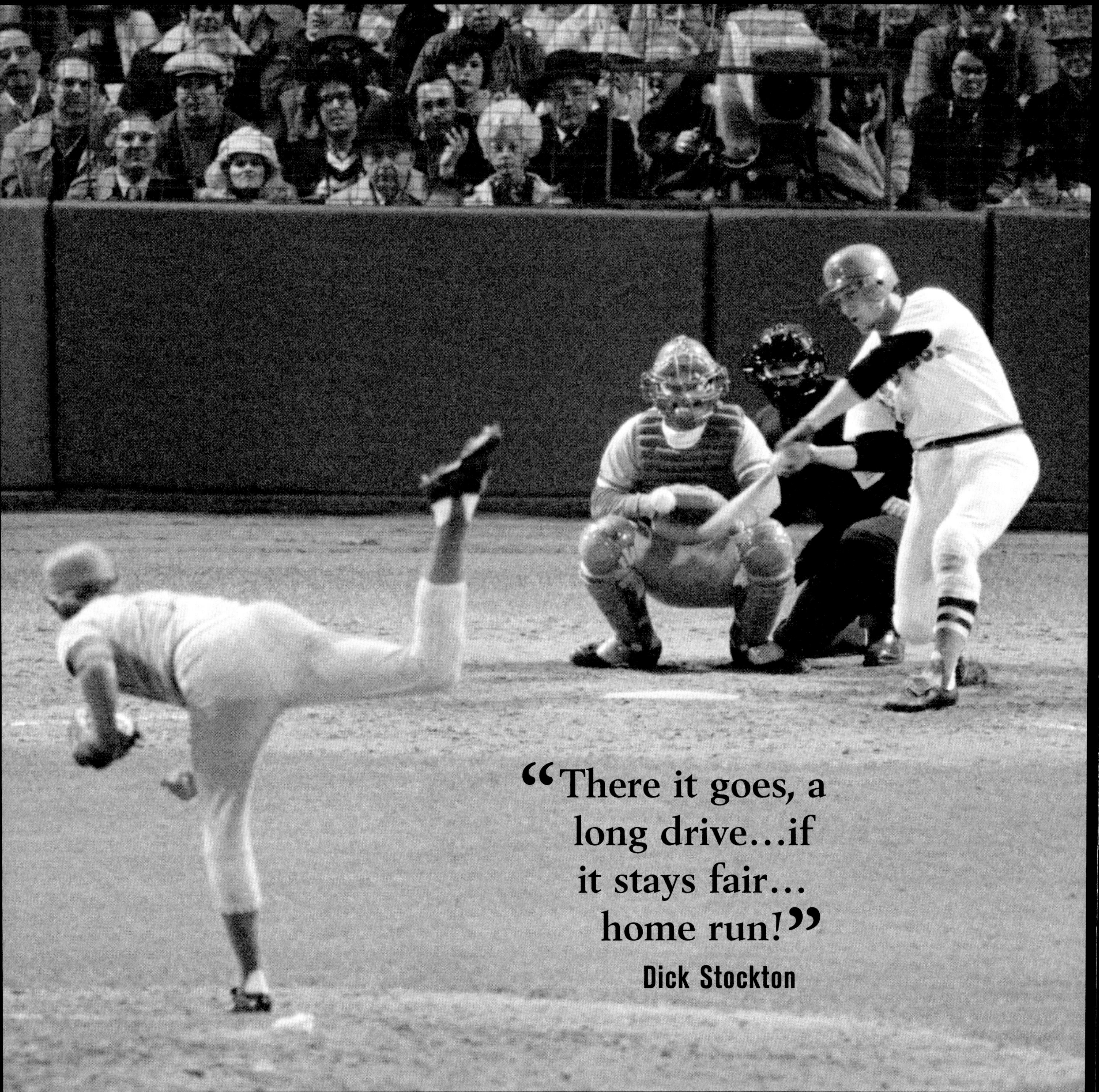

"There it goes, a
long drive…if
it stays fair…
home run!"

Dick Stockton

# Carlton Fisk Waves World Series Home Run Fair

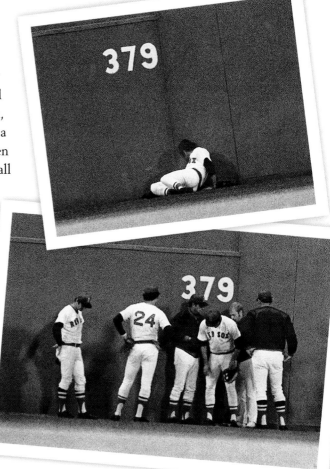

October 21, 1975, was not the final game of the World Series between the Boston Red Sox and the Cincinnati Reds. Nor was the winner of the game that year's world champion. Yet, the events of that night distinctly stand out from those of any other game in the series.

Boston and Cincinnati were both ravenous for a championship. The Reds had not won one since 1940, and the Red Sox had been waiting since 1918. Cincinnati was favored from the outset with its team of power and speed, which included Pete Rose, Joe Morgan, Johnny Bench, Tony Perez, Cesar Geronimo, Rawly Eastwick, and Ken Griffey Sr.

Though they were underdogs, the Red Sox weren't exactly pushovers. Manager Darrell Johnson's line-up card included the player with the league's highest slugging average, Fred Lynn, plus three other sluggers with .300+ batting averages: Carl Yastrzemski, Cecil Cooper, and Carlton "Pudge" Fisk.

Boston shocked Cincinnati in game one as pitcher Luis Tiant shut them out 6 to 0. The Reds came back to take games two and three; Boston eked out a win in game four; and Cincinnati came back again to win game five and go ahead 3 games to 2. One more win, and the Reds would have the championship. But first they had to fly back to Boston and beat the Red Sox in the friendly confines of Fenway Park.

In the first inning of game six, the Red Sox took a 3 to 0 lead when Fred Lynn homered off Reds starting pitcher Gary Nolan. Tiant pitched masterfully until the fifth inning, when he walked a man, Pete Rose singled, and Ken Griffey hit a carom shot off Fenway's infamous Green Monster—the thirty-seven-foot-high wall in left field. The ballpark suddenly was silent. In trying to field the ball, Lynn crashed into the wall and hurt his back. To everyone's relief, Lynn was able to finish the inning. But Tiant was struggling, and by the end of the fifth inning, the score was tied at three.

Johnson left Tiant in the game and, in the seventh inning, Cincinnati scored two more runs. Now the Reds were up 5 to 3. When Reds slugger Cesar Geronimo led off the eighth with a homer just inside the right field foul pole, Johnson pulled Tiant from the game. Boston came back in the bottom of the eighth inning when unlikely hero, Bernie Carbo, a .257 utility player, came in to pinch hit. With two men on base and two men out, Carbo smashed a Rawly Eastwick pitch over the center field fence, tying the game at six.

*(clockwise from left) Carlton Fisk hits his game-winning homer. ■ Boston's Fred Lynn slumps to the ground after making a crucial catch that sent him crashing into the wall. ■ Red Sox manager Darrell Johnson and trainer Charlie Moss examine Lynn.*

(above) Fisk hits his game-winning 12th-inning home run. ■ (right) The Red Sox catcher attempts to wave his home run fair, then celebrates as it stays inside the left field foul pole.

Regulation play ended with that same score, and on went game six into extra innings. Both teams held fast—nobody scored through eleven. But in the top of the 11<sup>th</sup>, the Red Sox got a scare. With Ken Griffey on base, Joe Morgan stroked a sure line-drive home run. Boston outfielder Dwight Evans made a spectacular lunging catch to rob Morgan of his homer, then, to top it off, fired the ball back to the infield, doubling up Griffey and ending the inning.

By the bottom of the 12<sup>th</sup>, it was after midnight. Boston's catcher and former Rookie of the Year, Carlton Fisk, stepped into the batters box against Reds reliever Pat Darcy. Just moments before, Fisk had experienced a small revelation. He said it was "one of those feelings you get that something is afoot." He turned to Lynn, who followed him in the order, and said, "Fred, I'm going to hit one off the wall. Drive me in."

After taking a ball, Fisk did even better than his prediction—he drove the next pitch deep to left. It was high and curling. One look and he knew—this ball was either going foul, or it was a home run. Fisk took a couple of dawdling steps toward first, never really taking his eyes off the ball as it soared to its uncertain destination. Then he stopped to watch the ball. But he didn't just watch, he began to jump and wave his arms frantically, pushing the air, trying to keep the ball from going foul. Red Sox fans held their breath, hoping for this one sign that their years of futility might be coming to an end. The ball obeyed Fisk's command and stayed fair.

In the broadcast booth for NBC Television was veteran announcer Dick Stockton, commenting on the three home runs hit that evening. Calling the moment, Stockton shouted, "There it goes, a long drive…if it stays fair…home run!"

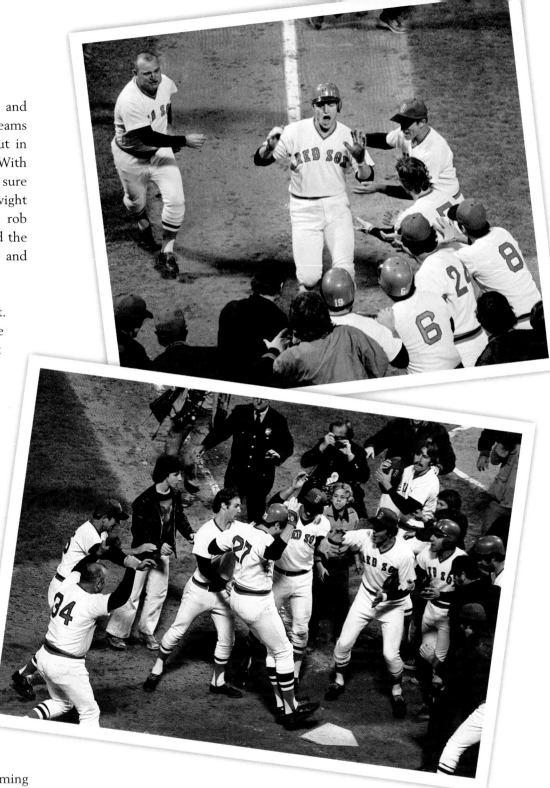

Carlton Fisk had won game six for Boston. Although the Boston Red Sox lost the Series the next day, they will forever remain the winners of one of the most dramatic games in World Series history. Reds manager Sparky Anderson, a man who'd seen many games, said of game six, "I've never seen a better one."

*Fisk is greeted by teammates as he reaches home plate.*

"The first time I have ever seen that in Olympic competition…a perfect ten!"

Cathy Rigby

# Nadia Comaneci Scores a Perfect 10

At the 1976 Summer Olympic Games in Montreal, fourteen-year-old Nadia Comaneci stood less than five feet tall and weighed just eighty-six pounds. Yet, this pint-sized, dark-eyed Romanian gymnast did something that no one had ever done before—she achieved perfection. In the process, she captured the hearts of the viewing public and pushed the sport of gymnastics to a new level of worldwide attention.

Integral to Comaneci's success was her legendary coach, Bela Karolyi, and his wife Marta, who found the young gymnast in her hometown of Onesti, a factory town nestled in the mountains of Romania. When Comaneci was only six years old, the Karolyis began training the nimble young athlete in gymnastics. Comaneci trained hard, mixing her school work with her expanding prowess in the gym. Her efforts paid off quickly.

At age eight, Comaneci was chosen to compete at the 1970 Romanian National Championships. She won the all-around title for her age group in both of the next two years. In 1975, she graduated to senior competitions. She entered the European championships and won three individual events and the all-around title.

In 1976, Comaneci made her first trip to the United States to compete in the inaugural American Cup meet, a competition that would be doubly memorable for the fourteen-year-old. At the meet in New York's Madison Square Garden, Comaneci not only scored a perfect 10 on one of her vaults, but she also met American gymnast Bart Conner, the man whom, twenty years later, she would marry.

Then came the Montreal Summer Olympic Games of 1976. The athlete to beat in women's gymnastics was the darling of the 1972 Munich Games, Russia's petite gold medal winner, Olga Korbut. Televised in the U.S. on ABC, coverage worked hard to establish a rivalry between Korbut and Comaneci, but it would never materialize. Korbut would capture only a silver— behind Comaneci's gold—on the balance beam in the individual events. While Korbut's Soviet squad did go on to win the women's team title, it was the 4-foot 11-inch Romanian who captivated the world and pulled her team to a second-place finish.

Comaneci's performance in her first compulsory exercise, the uneven bars, was unprecedented. After her dismount, the awed crowd waited in hushed anticipation for her score. Comaneci remembers, "I never looked at the scores. I judged

*(clockwise from left) Comaneci's flawless performance on the uneven bars rendered the first perfect 10. ■ Nadia Comaneci ■ Olga Korbut*

*(photos at left) Comaneci performs a perfect routine on the uneven bars.* ■ *(right) Comaneci stands in front of the scoreboard that shows her perfect 10, the first ever in Olympic competition.*

for myself and I thought I might have had a 9.9." But instead of a "9.9," a blazing "1.00" flashed on the board. There was a roar of surprise, then an enormous cheer as the crowd realized what the low number on the scoreboard meant: Comaneci was the first gymnast in Olympic history to score a perfect 10. And, as the event announcer explained to the crowd, the judges had to display a "1.00" on the board because the scoring system had been built to accommodate the highest score of only 9.9. Soon after, competitions around the world had to replace or remodel their scoring systems to include a perfect 10.

Comaneci proved to everyone that her score was no fluke. Later performing in the optional exercises, she scored her second and third perfect 10s on the uneven bars and the balance beam. Before the games were over, she was awarded four more perfect 10s, again on the uneven bars and balance

beam. While her remarkable seven perfect 10s captured the public's imagination, her overall medal count was just as impressive. Comaneci collected three gold medals, one silver, and one bronze, while winning the hearts of millions of fans across the globe.

Four years later, Comaneci was again center stage at the Olympics, this time in Moscow, Russia. Now older and taller, she wasn't able to repeat her astonishing performance of 1976, but she did win two gold medals and help her team snare the silver medal in the all-around competition.

As Communism crumbled in Eastern Europe, Comaneci defected from Romania and was granted asylum in the United States. On Bart Conner's invitation, she joined him as a teacher in his gymnastics academy in Norman, Oklahoma, and in 1996, the two gold medal winners married.

*(photos at left) Comaneci's balance beam performance earned her a third perfect 10. ■ (right) Comaneci shows off her gold.*

"It's all over!
Michigan State University,
National Champions, 1979!"
Dick Enberg

# Johnson vs. Bird in the NCAA Championship

In the late 1970s, interest in college and professional basketball was stagnant at best, and in many areas declining. The National Basketball Association suffered from a lack of team play, both on offense and defense. College basketball was in search of stars and top teams following the UCLA dynasty years of 1964 to 1975.

Beginning with the 1978-79 college basketball season, however, Earvin "Magic" Johnson from Michigan State University and Indiana State's Larry Bird began to change all that. Together, they gave an immediate boost to college basketball, and their rivalry led the NBA to unprecedented popularity during the 1980s.

It would be easy to say their rivalry was sparked by their differences, but Larry Bird and Magic Johnson were more alike than different.

Neither was exceptionally quick and neither was a great leaper. But both were great passers with tremendous court sense and vision. Both would put the ball in the hands of an open teammate instead of taking a jump shot while guarded. Both were fiercely competitive. Johnson was a better ball handler, Bird the superior shooter. Most importantly, both made every player on their respective teams better, and in the process, made their teams as a whole better. Under the leadership of Bird and Johnson, the emphasis was back on team basketball.

Bird led the Indiana State Sycamores to an undefeated 1978-79 regular season. They easily won the Missouri Valley Conference and qualified for the NCAA tournament.

Magic Johnson and the Michigan State Spartans struggled at first. Eight games into the Big Ten conference schedule, they had four wins and four losses, including a humiliating eighteen-point loss to Northwestern University, the worst team in the conference. In 1979, forty teams were invited to the NCAA tournament, and it looked like Michigan State would not be one of them. But the Spartans rallied during the second half of the conference schedule, winning all but one game, and they were on their way to the NCAA tournament.

Both Michigan State and Indiana State emerged victorious from their first four tournament games. As many fans had hoped, the championship game would feature a highly anticipated Bird–Johnson match-up.

On March 26, 1979, the nation turned to their television sets in record numbers to watch the first meeting of what became one of the greatest rivalries in all of sports. Unfortunately, the game did not

*(left to right) Larry Bird reaches for a loose ball while Magic Johnson (33) rushes downcourt.* ■ *Johnson and Bird speak to the press before the game.*

*(clockwise from upper left) Johnson sets for a layup. ■ Michigan State players go all out to defend against Bird. ■ Bird struggles to escape a Michigan State double-team. ■ Johnson and Bird fall to the floor.*

live up to the hype. Michigan State employed its typical match-up zone defense, but with an added attraction. Bird was constantly double-teamed by the Spartans and the heavy coverage frustrated him. Indiana State struggled and the Spartans enjoyed a double-digit lead throughout most of the game. They got typically strong offensive output from Johnson and co-star Greg Kelser, but, in the second half, Kelser received his fourth foul and was forced to go to the bench.

With one of the Spartans' leaders out, Indiana State cut the lead to six points with ten minutes to play. But, when Kelser came back into the game,

Michigan State once again assumed control. In the closing seconds, as they had done countless times in their college careers, Johnson hit Kelser with a full-court pass for a slam dunk. Michigan State won 75 to 64. Bird finished the game having made just seven field goals in twenty-one attempts and scoring nineteen points, below his normal output. Johnson finished with twenty-four points, seven rebounds, and five assists.

Televised on NBC, the game received the highest Nielsen television rating ever for an NCAA tournament game. The nation witnessed the birth of a rivalry and, in many ways, the rebirth of basketball.

*(upper left) Johnson raises his arms in victory. ■ (upper right) Johnson waves to fans at the Michigan State victory parade. ■ (center) Bird talks to his coach on the sidelines. ■ (bottom) Johnson performs the traditional cutting of the net.*

"Do you believe in miracles? Yes!"
Al Michaels

# U.S. Hockey Team Defeats Soviet Union

In the year before the 1980 Winter Olympics in Lake Placid, New York, United States coach Herb Brooks began to assemble his team. Brooks wanted a team of young college kids who would play the Soviet style of hockey, with more passing, weaving, and free skating than the physical style played in the National Hockey League. He also wanted the best-conditioned team in the Olympics. After selecting his roster, Brooks relentlessly pushed his players with stamina-building drills for six months.

But even with a fast, well-conditioned team, the chances of beating the Soviet Union in the Olympics were highly improbable, if not impossible. After all, this was the same Soviet team that defeated the NHL All-Stars in the Challenge Cup one year earlier. During the week before the Olympic Games, the U.S. played their final exhibition game against the Soviet Union, which the Soviets won 10 to 3.

America's first hockey game in the 1980 Olympics came on February 12, against the favored Swedish team. Bill Baker scored for the U.S. with twenty-seven seconds left to give America a 2 to 2 tie, an emotional, come-from-behind game that set the tone for the rest of the Olympic hockey tournament. The U.S. followed with a string of victories: 7 to 3 over Czechoslovakia; 5 to 1 over Norway; 7 to 2 over Romania; and 4 to 2 over West Germany.

The U.S. hockey team already had exceeded expectations and was building momentum for a showdown against the Soviet Union, winners of every Olympic hockey gold medal since 1964.

The U.S.A. met the U.S.S.R on Friday, February 22, 1980, in the first semifinal game of the tournament. The Soviets had breezed through the tournament with five wins and no losses. The cold war rivalry generated tremendous excitement. Although the game had a 5 P.M. eastern time start, the ABC television network opted to televise the game on tape delay in prime time where it could be seen by the largest audience.

By the time the game took place, the U.S. team was on such a roll, their earlier defeat to the Soviets seemed like ancient history. In his speech before the game, Coach Brooks assured his players that they were no fluke, and could beat the Soviets.

In the first period, the Soviets took a quick 2 to 1 lead and held a commanding advantage in shots on goal, but with one second to play in the period, American center Mark Johnson scored to tie the game at two. The concerned Soviets changed goalies, taking out Vladislav Tretiak and replacing him with Vladimir Myshkin. Action in the second period was much like the first, with the Soviets

*(left to right) U.S. players crowd the ice to celebrate just moments after defeating the Soviet Union. ■ U.S. center Rob McClanahan takes a shot against Soviet goalie Vladimir Myshkin.*

dominating. They out-shot the Americans 12 to 2, but got only one goal to take a 3 to 2 lead into the third period.

Throughout the tournament, the Americans had started slowly but finished strong because of their superb conditioning. This game was no exception. At 8:39 of the third period, Johnson tied the game at three on a power play. Less than a minute and a half later, American Mike Eruzione picked up the puck, skated into the slot, and put a wrist shot past Myshkin for a 4 to 3 U.S. lead. With ten minutes to play, the Americans led by one and the Soviets appeared tired. The Americans continued to skate well, and goaltender Jim Craig turned away the rest of the Soviet shots.

ABC announcer Al Michaels, who was above the action in the broadcast booth, later recalled, "The arena was so loud, the emotion so great. Everybody was going crazy. I remember thinking, 'Stay with it. Don't get swept up.' The hotter it gets, the cooler you have to get. I remember thinking of one word in my mind—'miraculous.'"

*(clockwise from bottom left) A skirmish erupts between the U.S. and Soviet teams. ■ Russia's Valery Kharlamov (17) and U.S. defenseman Bill Baker collide during the semifinal game. ■ Neal Broten attempts a shot against Norway. ■ After helping lead his team to a gold medal, U.S. goalie Jim Craig holds the flag while searching the stands for his father.*

The game wound down to its final seconds. The U.S. players passed the puck and Michaels began the countdown, "Eleven seconds, you got ten seconds, the countdown going on right now. Morrow up to Silk. Five seconds left in the game. Do you believe in miracles? Yes!"

The victory over the Soviets seemed climactic, but the U.S. still had one more game left to play. Although not assured of any medal if they lost, they could capture the gold if they beat Finland.

On Sunday morning, February 24, 1980, the U.S. took to the ice to battle Finland for the gold. Like the other games in this tournament, Team U.S.A. fell behind early, trailing 2 to 1 going into the third period. But once again, the American team dominated play in the final period. Forward Phil Verchota tied the game early in the period. Center Rob McClanahan gave the U.S. a 3 to 2 lead with fourteen minutes to play and Johnson added an insurance goal with 3:35 to play.

The United States won 4 to 2 over Finland and captured the gold medal. The arena erupted with cheers of "U.S.A.! U.S.A!" One of many images of the celebration etched into viewers' memories is that of American goalie Jim Craig wrapped in the American flag, looking into the stands and searching for his father.

Later that night, the celebration at Lake Placid concluded with the medals ceremony and the singing of the United States National Anthem. Captain Mike Eruzione stood alone on the victory platform while his teammates stood at attention at the blue line. When the singing concluded, Eruzione waved to all his teammates to join him on the platform to show the nation their hockey medals. A hockey team and a nation celebrated.

*(top to bottom) The U.S. team celebrates on the ice after winning the gold medal. ■ Captain Mike Eruzione, center, stands alone on the victory podium as the American flag is raised. The U.S. team stands at the blue line ready to join him. ■ The American team gathers on the victory stand during the medals ceremony.*

"Bjorn has won it!"
Bud Collins

# Bjorn Borg Defeats John McEnroe at Wimbledon

In 1980, the tennis world was captivated by two powerful performers: Bjorn Borg, a twenty-four-year-old, seemingly invincible winner of four consecutive Wimbledon titles; and John McEnroe, a twenty-one-year-old American tennis star dubbed "superbrat" by the international press. Together in the men's finals at Wimbledon, the two would stage a five-set, nearly four-hour marathon bout that would have tennis fans talking for years.

Borg was riding a record thirty-four-match winning streak at Wimbledon. McEnroe had just ousted Jimmy Connors in the semifinals to reach the Wimbledon finals for the first time in his career. Vilified by the London tabloid, *The Sun*, as the "most ill-tempered, petulant loudmouth that the game of tennis has ever known," McEnroe entered Centre Court on July 5, 1980, to loud booing from the sixteen thousand fans in attendance.

McEnroe started the match in control, winning the first set 6-1 in just twenty minutes. Borg battled back, winning the hotly contested second set 7-5, and then breezed through the third set, winning 6-3. With Borg leading two sets to one, the two embarked on a dramatic fourth-set battle that became a part of Wimbledon legend.

The set began with both players winning the games in which they served. But with the score tied at four games each, Borg broke McEnroe's serve to take a 5 games to 4 lead. In the tenth game, Borg took the lead, and with the score 40-15, he was serving match point.

But McEnroe would not be dismissed so easily. He fought off the first match point with a strong backhand, then the second with a drop shot, forcing the game to deuce. Two points later, McEnroe completed his service break. The set was tied at five and he had come back from nearly certain defeat. The crowd that began the match jeering and shouting at him exploded into cheers as McEnroe let out a victorious yell.

Borg and McEnroe split the next two games to tie the set at six and force a tiebreaker. The first player to win seven points, and win by a two-point margin, would win the set. For Borg, winning the set would earn him the match. In the tiebreaker, Borg held match points with a 6-5 lead and a 7-6 lead, but McEnroe held on to tie both times.

*(left to right) Borg falls to his knees after defeating McEnroe for his fifth straight Wimbledon title.* ■ *Borg in action during the 1980 Wimbledon title match*

The set continued as a remarkable test of endurance and nerves, with McEnroe fighting off five match points and Borg surviving six set points. But with the score 17-16 in McEnroe's favor, Borg could hold out no longer. McEnroe was finally successful at a set point, winning the tiebreaker 18-16, and tying the match at two sets each.

The dramatic tiebreaker had lasted an amazing twenty-two minutes, longer than it had taken McEnroe to win the entire first set, and the crowd was exhilarated. Now, one final set would decide the 1980 Wimbledon men's champion.

Both players continued their strong serving records in the fifth set, with each winning the games they served until the score came to 7-6 in Borg's favor. The final set at Wimbledon has no tiebreaker, meaning a player must win by two games, so the match continued.

Though McEnroe served the 14th game of the final set, Borg had command of the game and began to turn the tables. The defending Wimbledon champ took the score to 15-40, double match point—his eighth match point of the day. This time, there would be no comeback for McEnroe. Three hours and fifty-three minutes after the match began, Borg sent a backhand past McEnroe to win his fifth straight Wimbledon men's singles title.

Falling to his knees on the grass of Centre Court, Bjorn Borg leaned back, clenched his fists in

*(top to bottom) John McEnroe*
■ *Bjorn Borg*

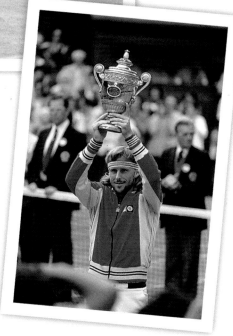

celebration, and looked to the sky. It's an image forever etched into the minds of the fans who witnessed the epic match. The Wimbledon crowd rewarded Borg and McEnroe with a two-minute standing ovation as the exhausted champion and challenger walked off.

Later in 1980, McEnroe beat Borg in the finals of the U.S. Open, beginning the passing of the champion's torch from one tennis superstar to the next. Then in 1981, McEnroe beat Borg in the Wimbledon finals, ending Borg's streak at five Wimbledon titles in a row. After the 1981 season, Borg retired from tennis at the age of twenty-five. McEnroe would go on to win a total of three Wimbledon titles and four U.S. Opens.

*(clockwise from bottom left) McEnroe, infamous for his on-court tantrums, displayed only the occasional outburst, and by doing so, won over Wimbledon spectators. ■ Borg celebrates his victory in front of a cheering crowd. ■ Borg holds up his Wimbledon trophy.*

"Dwight Clark has it! It's a touchdown for the 49ers!"

Don Klein

# "The Catch": 49ers vs. Cowboys

In 1981, Joe Montana's first year as a starting quarterback, the San Francisco 49ers posted the best record in the National Football League, thirteen wins and three losses, an amazing turnaround from the 6 and 10 season the year before.

More than sixty thousand fans crowded San Francisco's Candlestick Park to watch the up-and-coming 49ers and the veteran Dallas Cowboys square off for the NFC championship on January 10, 1982.

The two teams traded scores for the first half and by the third quarter, the 49ers had the lead. But in the fourth quarter, Dallas came back with a field goal and took a 27 to 21 lead on a twenty-one-yard touchdown pass from Danny White to Doug Cosbie.

With 4:54 left in the fourth quarter, the 49ers began a drive at their own eleven-yard line, eighty-nine yards away from victory. Through a series of passes and runs, they methodically made their way up the field to the Cowboys' six-yard line. It was third down with three yards to go and a scant fifty-eight seconds remaining on the clock.

On the snap, Montana rolled to his right. His intended receiver was Freddie Solomon, but he was covered. Meanwhile, a Cowboys' pass rush was closing in on Montana.

Falling backward and throwing off his back foot, Montana heaved the ball to the back of the end zone toward 6-foot 4-inch wide receiver Dwight Clark. Cowboys defensive back Everson Walls was covering Clark, but suddenly stopped. The ball was thrown so high Walls thought it was going out-of-bounds and Clark wouldn't be able to grasp it.

The taller Clark leapt high for the ball, caught it on his fingertips, and just barely planted his feet in bounds for the touchdown.

The crowd at Candlestick Park went into a frenzy. Ray Wersching kicked the extra point to give the 49ers a 28 to 27 lead. San Francisco held on for the final few seconds to win the game and their first trip to the Super Bowl.

Clark's game-winning grab has been forever termed by sports fans as simply "The Catch." Although some believe that Montana was just trying to throw the ball out of the end zone and Clark got in the way, Clark insists it was a play they had practiced often.

Two weeks later, the 49ers beat the Cincinnati Bengals in Pontiac, Michigan, 26 to 21 in Super Bowl XVI. It was the first of four Super Bowl victories for Joe Montana and the 49ers in a nine-year span.

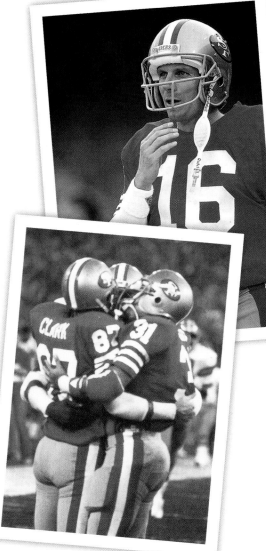

*(clockwise from left) Dwight Clark makes a fingertip catch to win the NFC championship.* ■ *Joe Montana* ■ *Teammate Walt Easley congratulates Dwight Clark in the end zone.*

"He held on in the closest finish in the history of the Indianapolis 500!"

Jim McKay

# Gordon Johncock Wins 1982 Indianapolis 500

The Indianapolis 500 is billed as the "Greatest Spectacle in Auto Racing." It's the biggest single-day sporting event in the world, drawing more than four hundred thousand fans to the Indianapolis Motor Speedway every Memorial Day weekend. Since 1911, the best drivers in the fastest cars have come to Indy to run two hundred laps around the two-and-one-half-mile track in search of auto racing's most cherished prize, the Borg-Warner Trophy.

The Indianapolis 500 is a long, grueling auto race, but in 1982, the marathon 500 became a sprint in the final thirteen laps between two drivers, Gordon Johncock and Rick Mears.

At forty-five, Johncock was a veteran Indy racer. He won the rain-shortened Indy 500 in 1973, but he was considered a hard luck driver with several near misses at winning a full Indy. Mears was a rising young star, having won the race in 1979. He also had the fastest car in the time trials preceding the May 30, 1982, race.

For the first 155 laps, Johncock's car didn't handle well but he managed to stay in contention in fourth place. But from lap 155 to lap 187, his car started to respond. He closed the gap on the leaders, and by virtue of a faster final pit stop than Mears, Johncock took over first place and had an eleven-second lead with thirteen laps to go.

That's when it started to go wrong for Johncock. His car started to handle poorly again and his left rear tire overheated, causing his car to push out in the turns. Johncock kept an eye on his rearview mirror watching Mears, clearly in the faster car, gain on him at the rate of one second per lap. With an average speed of 197 m.p.h., Mears had closed the gap, leaving no cars between his and Johncock's.

With five laps remaining, Mears was charging at Johncock at the speed of 199 m.p.h. and was just 4.6 seconds back. Johncock was running first, followed by Mears, with Tom Sneva trailing in third place. Just three laps from the checkered flag that signaled the end of the race, the exhaust of Sneva's Texaco Star began puffing white smoke. Both drivers and spectators feared a yellow caution flag would end the excitement, but Sneva managed to steer his ailing car into the pit and fourth-place Pancho Carter moved into third.

*(left to right) Gordon Johncock is followed closely by Rick Mears in the 1982 Indy 500. ■ Johncock basks in the glory of his first Indy 500 win in 1973.*

By lap 198, Johncock held the lead by a precariously thin three-quarters of a second, and at almost 200 m.p.h., Mears closed the margin to within seventy-five yards of Johncock. As the two drivers came to the white flag signaling the final lap, Mears pulled even with Johncock, but Johncock held him off in the first turn, the second turn, the back stretch, and the third turn.

Legendary sportscaster Jim McKay was calling the race for ABC Sports. His excitement in the booth mirrored that of the fans in the grandstand, especially as Mears and Johncock were coming out of the fourth turn into the home stretch toward the checkered flag. "Can he make a move at the finish?" McKay asked. As Mears bounced to the outside and tried to pass Johncock, McKay shouted, "He's making a move! No! No! Not quite!" John-

cock held him off and crossed the finish line 0.16 seconds, or slightly more than a car length, in front of Mears. "Gordon Johncock has won it! He held on in the closest finish in the history of the Indianapolis 500!" exclaimed McKay.

Pancho Carter crossed the finish line one lap behind Mears, taking third, followed by Sneva, who had accumulated enough laps before having to take himself out of the race, with Al Unser Sr. rounding out the top five.

Gordon Johncock had finally won his first full Indianapolis 500, and continued racing for ten more years. Rick Mears fulfilled predictions of greatness and went on to win three more Indy 500s, tying him with A.J. Foyt Jr. and Al Unser Sr. with four Indy victories.

(opposite page, left to right) The start of the 1982 Indy 500 ■ Johncock's car

(top to bottom) Johncock crosses the finish line barely more than a car length ahead of Mears. ■ Johncock celebrates his victory in the winner's circle, surrounded by fans, friends, and family.

"The most amazing, sensational, traumatic, heartrending, exciting, thrilling finish in the history of college football!"

Joe Starkey

# "The Play": Cal vs. Stanford

Out of the thousands of plays run since Rutgers met Princeton in the first intercollegiate football game in 1869, only one is known simply as "The Play." It was an event so out of the ordinary, one that was so weird and wonderful, that it needs no other name.

On November 20, 1982, 75,662 fans packed Memorial Stadium in Berkeley, California, where the University of California Golden Bears were playing the Stanford Cardinal, a game with its own inherent drama. It was their eighty-fifth meeting, and one of the West Coast's oldest and most bitter rivalries. It was the last game of the season, so a year's worth of bragging rights were on the line, along with an invitation to the postseason Hall of Fame Bowl and possession of The Axe.

The Axe first appeared in 1899, at a Cal–Stanford baseball game. The Stanford faithful were using it to cut blue and gold ribbons, Cal's colors, to taunt the Bears fans. Cal's fans were so infuriated, they stole The Axe. Eventually, officials from both schools met and decided The Axe would go to the football team that won the annual match-up.

The game was hard-fought and close throughout. Near the end of the fourth quarter, Cal held a 19 to 17 lead. With seconds ticking, Stanford quarterback and future NFL player John Elway engineered a long drive that left his team within field-goal

range with eight seconds left in the game. Stanford kicker Mark Harmon attempted a thirty-five-yard field goal, the ball split the uprights, and the referees signaled the successful kick. The clock showed only four seconds to go and Stanford was ahead 20 to 19. Cal play-by-play man Joe Starkey summed up the seemingly hopeless situation, saying, "Only a miracle can save the Bears."

With just four seconds left, there would be a kickoff, an unlikely return for a touchdown, the clock would run out, and the contest would be over. Stanford players on the sidelines celebrated the field goal and all-but-certain win by running onto the field, for which officials penalized them. The violation cost Stanford a fifteen-yard penalty, forcing them to kick from the twenty-five-yard line instead of up at the forty. The Stanford band headed for the end zone, ready to play their victory song when the four seconds were up. But they'd forgotten something—four seconds, four minutes, or four hours, the game doesn't end until the play is over and the referee's whistle blows.

In the Bears' huddle, strong safety Richard Rodgers called for a simple go-for-broke strategy, "If you're gonna get tackled, lateral the ball. I mean, don't fall with that ball." Meanwhile, the Stanford band had gathered in the end zone as Stanford kicked to Cal.

*(left to right) Cal's Kevin Moen celebrates his touchdown amongst stunned members of the Stanford band.*
■ *Stanford quarterback John Elway*

*(above) The end zone is overrun with fans and band members as Moen scores his touchdown. On the right, he barrels over Stanford trombone player Gary Tyrrell, who later received considerable media attention for his courageous block.*

When a Cal player picked up the ball, the crowd counted backwards from four to one. When the four seconds were up, the jubilant bandmembers rushed onto the field. But Cal was still playing out their kickoff return.

Stanford's kick hit the ground and bounced into the hands of Cal's Kevin Moen at his own forty-four-yard line. Moen started running, noticing Stanford strong safety Barry Cromer barreling towards him. Moen hurled an overhand pass to teammate Richard Rodgers at the Cal forty-six and then circled around behind Rodgers.

Rodgers was surprised by the pass but continued his charge up the field. Just before he was nearly picked off by Stanford cornerback Darrell Grissum, Rodgers pitched another lateral pass to Cal running back Dwight Garner. Garner took his first hit at the Cal forty-nine from Stanford linebacker David Wyman, but managed to stay in motion. Then, just before he was nearly tackled by linebacker Mark Andrew, Garner shovel-passed the ball back to Rodgers. From the Cal forty-eight-yard line, Rodgers started upfield for the second time with Moen and Cal wide receiver Mariet Ford running alongside him. With a Stanford player now directly in front of him, Rodgers lateraled to Ford. Three Cardinal defenders were waiting for Ford at the Stanford twenty-seven-yard line. Ford threw himself into the three Stanford players while at the same time tossing the ball over his shoulder. Moen managed to reach back and scoop up the fifth miraculous lateral toss at the Stanford twenty-five. All that was between him and the goal line was the 144-member Stanford band.

Moen ran down the Stanford sideline, sidestepped a tuba player, and ran through fifteen other band-members on his way to a touchdown. In the end zone, he ran smack into trombone player Gary Tyrrell and knocked him flat on his instrument. Someone from Stanford had finally stopped Kevin Moen—but it was too late. Fans listening to the game on KGO radio heard announcer Joe Starkey as he did his best to sum up the unbelievable finale: "Oh my God! The most amazing, sensational, traumatic, heartrending, exciting, thrilling finish in the history of college football!"

There was pandemonium on the field as officials decided whether the score would stand. The wild play was ruled a touchdown and the game was over. The California Golden Bears won 25 to 20. The game—and The Axe—was theirs.

To this day, every time The Axe changes hands, the school that has it changes the final score of the 1982 game inscribed on it. When Stanford possesses it, the score is 20 to 19, and when Cal has it, the score is 25 to 20.

*(top to bottom) In winning the Big Game, Cal also won rights to "The Axe," a traveling trophy that has been awarded to the champion of the annual match-up since 1930. ■ Jubilant Cal players and fans celebrate their victory.*

"The Cinderella
team has done it!
The glass slipper fits!"
Wally Ausley

# NC State Upsets Houston

North Carolina State came into the 1983 NCAA men's basketball tournament facing seemingly impossible odds. During the regular season, the Wolfpack had suffered ten losses, more than any NCAA champion in history. And if that wasn't enough, after fighting their way to the championship game, the team they were up against was the No. 1 team in the nation, the University of Houston Cougars. The Cougars were a powerhouse team with an athletic, slam-dunking style that earned them the nickname "Phi Slamma Jamma."

The talent behind Houston's flash was future NBA superstars Hakeem [Akeem] Olajuwon and Clyde Drexler. Between them, they put on a season-long aerial show the likes of which had never been seen at the college level.

North Carolina State's star, on the other hand, was its coach. Jim Valvano's loud and proud presence on the basketball court was second only to his command of game strategy. That year especially, Valvano was an event unto himself. Arriving at the tournament in Albuquerque, New Mexico, he stepped off the plane, waded into the throng of reporters waiting for him, announced, "Welcome to the Jim Valvano Show," and predicted a tournament victory. The North Carolina State team backed up their coach's bold prediction, defeating the University of Georgia in the Final Four to play for the championship.

In the North Carolina State locker room before the final game, Valvano did one of the things he did best; he motivated his team, saying, "Now people say Houston will kill us. Someone wrote that elephants will ride in the Indy 500 and Orson Welles will not eat breakfast, lunch, or dinner before NC State beats Houston. Well, we're going to attack, press, and go hard at them all over, all the time. We will not let them dunk. We will dunk and we will win!"

It's no surprise the game started with a dunk. But fans didn't anticipate it would be North Carolina State with the lead-off slam. The first two points of the game were scored by North Carolina State forward Thurl Bailey. As the game got rolling, Valvano's strategy revealed itself. His team took control of the game by slowing down the tempo. They crowded the Cougars around the basket, not letting them inside where they could dunk. In fact, Houston didn't get a single dunk until the fifteen-minute mark of the first half. Lacking strong outside shooting, the shocked Houston team trailed 33 to 25 at halftime.

*(left to right) NC State forward Lorenzo Charles slam dunks to win the NCAA championship. ■ Wolfpack forward Thurl Bailey fights off heavy defense from Houston's Larry Michaeux (40) and David Rose. Bailey led NC State in scoring with fifteen points.*

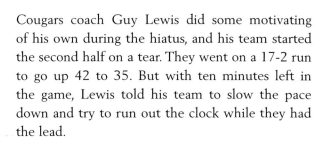

Cougars coach Guy Lewis did some motivating of his own during the hiatus, and his team started the second half on a tear. They went on a 17-2 run to go up 42 to 35. But with ten minutes left in the game, Lewis told his team to slow the pace down and try to run out the clock while they had the lead.

Valvano countered by instructing his players to foul the Cougars. He wanted the Houston team on the free-throw line—they had only about a 60 percent free-throw average for the season. The scheme worked perfectly. While Houston's free throws rattled off the rim, the Wolfpack climbed back into the game, and with 1:59 to play, NC State guard Dereck Whittenburg hit a jump shot to tie the score at 52. Houston got the ball and the Wolfpack once again fouled, putting Cougars guard Alvin Franklin on the line. He missed the first shot and possession went to the Wolfpack.

*(top to bottom) Bailey dunks the ball during NC State's 54-52 win over Houston.* ■ *NC State coach Jim Valvano waves the net in celebration of his team's upset victory over Houston.*

(top to bottom) *Valvano embraces Charles after his game-winning basket.* ■ *Valvano displays the NCAA championship trophy amid a crowd during the victory celebration.*

Coach Valvano's team brought the ball down the floor, and with the score tied, played for the last shot. With the clock down to five seconds, Houston deflected a Thurl Bailey pass. But the Wolfpack's Whittenburg retrieved it, and with the clock ticking down to zero, he turned and hoisted a desperate thirty-foot-plus jumper toward the basket. It was short.

Although Houston's Olajuwon was within range of recovering the ball and sending the game into overtime, he never jumped to retrieve it. Wolfpack forward Lorenzo Charles sneaked in behind Olajuwon, grabbed the shot out of the air, and stuffed it into the basket. The buzzer sounded and the Wolfpack had pulled off one of the greatest upsets in college basketball history.

**"It's just nose-to-tail on the back straightaway."**

Barney Hall

# Richard Petty Wins 200th Career Race

Some historic sports achievements happen all in an afternoon—a Hail Mary pass for a touchdown, a buzzer-beater to win in overtime, a homer in the bottom of the ninth inning. Some achievements take an entire career—Carl Lewis' nine Olympic gold medals, Hank Aaron's 755 home runs. It's an exceedingly rare occasion when the two converge. But that's just what happened on July 4, 1984, at Daytona Beach, Florida.

Richard Petty, from Level Cross, North Carolina, had been up to his ears in axle grease since he was old enough to hold a crescent wrench. Legend has it that by age ten, he could take an engine apart and put it back together. By the time he was thirteen, he was part of his dad's pit crew as they ran the NASCAR circuit. When Richard announced to his father, three-time NASCAR champion Lee Petty, that he wanted to go into racing, it certainly wasn't a surprise.

Richard Petty began his racing career July 12, 1958, just ten days past his 21st birthday. He entered nine races that year and his highest finish was a sixth place at a half-mile clay track in Columbia, South Carolina. Even though he'd won only $760 that season, Petty was back for more in 1959. And at that same Columbia track, he collected his very first victory. He captured his first NASCAR circuit victory the next year at the Charlotte Speedway.

Over the next quarter-century, Petty roared to records that some today consider unbeatable. In 1967, his best year, "King Richard" entered forty-eight races and won an incredible twenty-seven, the most ever in a NASCAR season. His career also includes 126 pole positions—another record expected never to be broken.

By the time Petty rolled across the starting line in the 1984 Firecracker 400, he'd captured the NASCAR championship an incredible seven times while racking up 199 wins. By comparison, his closest competitor was driver David Pearson, who had just more than one hundred wins. Petty's anticipated 200th win drew a large crowd, including President Ronald Reagan, the first sitting U.S. president to attend a NASCAR race.

With just twenty laps remaining in the 160-lap race, the lead had narrowed to two of stock car racing's most experienced pilots—Petty and skilled veteran Cale Yarborough. They were a decisive twenty-five seconds ahead of the pack. Petty was in the lead, and Yarborough was inches away from his back bumper, drafting him, waiting for the moment he could use Petty's aerodynamics to slingshot his own car into the lead.

*(clockwise from left) Petty wins his 200th race by just a car length. ■ President Ronald Reagan, center, accepts a banner with the signatures of Firecracker drivers. Reagan was the first sitting president to attend a NASCAR race. ■ Petty's #43 car*

Another eighteen laps rolled by, and Petty's masterful driving would not allow Yarborough any kind of an opening to get by him. Then, with just two laps to go, rookie driver Doug Heveron lost control of his car and spun out onto the apron of the racetrack at turn one. That brought out the yellow caution flag. Both drivers knew that since no passing was allowed after they reached the flagstand, the first driver to the caution flag would be the race winner. Petty later remembered, "That essentially turned lap 158 into the last lap….I took off and so did Cale."

The crowd of eighty thousand knew what was happening, and with a huge roar, rose to their feet to watch two miles of do-or-die drag racing. Calling the action on radio for the Motor Racing Network were anchors Eli Gold, Mike Joy, and thirty-year veteran Barney Hall. "It's Richard Petty. He revs up the STP Pontiac…Yarborough hounding him. It's just nose-to-tail on the back straightaway."

In turn three, Yarborough used the slingshot effect to shoot past Petty and grab the lead. But it was only momentary. Yarborough dove to the inside and ran beside Petty as they hit the third turn. Entering turn four, their positions reversed. When they emerged from the turn and onto the final straightaway, they were neck and neck, fender to fender at 200 m.p.h. As they jockeyed for the lead, the two cars bounced off one another several times and at the last possible moment, Petty's #43 car surged ahead to beat Yarborough to the flag. Yarborough pulled off the racetrack and into pit road before completing lap 160, thinking the race was over at that point. The mistake cost him second place, and he officially fell to third place behind driver Harry Gant who had been more than a mile behind Petty and Yarborough.

Richard Petty had won his 200th NASCAR victory. He raced for another eight years, but never won again. In 1992, after 1,185 races, King Richard abdicated his throne, parked #43, and hung up his racing suit for good.

(opposite page, top to bottom) Yarborough leads Petty in the third turn of the 158th lap, but at the fourth turn, Petty is able to swing into the lead. Petty finished the last lap before the yellow caution flag only a car-length ahead of Yarborough.

(at left) Petty takes the checkered flag to win. ■ (above) Petty and his crew receive the Firecracker 400 trophy and the attention of adoring fans.

"I don't believe it!
It's a touchdown!
The Eagles win it!"

Brent Musburger

# Boston College Beats Miami on Hail Mary Pass

The exact day the term "Hail Mary" left the dominion of the Catholic religion and came to describe a desperate, final-second pass is not known. But after November 23, 1984, Boston College quarterback Doug Flutie had practically redefined the term.

The game was a perfect Thanksgiving weekend match-up, the University of Miami Hurricanes, led by quarterback Bernie Kosar, versus Flutie's Boston College Eagles. Boston College came into the game with a record of 7-2, its most successful season since 1942. Miami held a record of 8-3, and were the defending national champions.

Despite wet and windy conditions at Miami's Orange Bowl stadium, with star passers on both squads, the game was an aerial show. The lead changed hands several times, with Boston College taking a three-point advantage into the final minutes. But just twenty-eight seconds away from a Boston College victory, Kosar led Miami to the end zone and a 45 to 41 lead.

Boston College received the ball, and Flutie managed to move his team forward thirty-two yards in three plays. Six seconds remained on the clock, and it was Boston College's ball on Miami's forty-eight-yard line. Flutie called for a "Hail Mary," a play in which all of his receivers were to converge in the end zone at the same time.

Flutie took the snap and was quickly chased out of the pocket to his right, which gave his receivers the time they needed to get to the end zone. Gerard Phelan, Flutie's ace receiver, was streaking upfield past Miami defender Darrell Fullington, who did little to stop him. "He must have thought Doug couldn't throw it that far," Phelan later remarked.

Flutie's pass traveled sixty-four yards, a remarkably long distance, especially into the wind and the rain. In the end zone, Phelan went up for the ball with Fullington, who had recovered and caught up with him. But Fullington mistimed his jump, and on the way up, was bumped by one of his own teammates. The ball passed right through their arms and Phelan pulled it in and fell to the turf in the end zone.

Boston College had upset the mighty University of Miami 47 to 45. Doug Flutie—who would go on to win the Heisman Trophy and play in the Canadian Football League and in the NFL for the Chicago Bears, the New England Patriots, and the Buffalo Bills—was the possessor of one of the most dramatic victories in college sports.

*(left to right) Doug Flutie scrambles out of the reach of Miami's Jerome Brown to complete a second-quarter pass. ■ Boston College's Darren Flutie congratulates his brother and teammate.*

"Jack Nicklaus has just won his sixth Masters. What a tournament!"

Pat Summerall

# Jack Nicklaus Wins Masters at Age 46

With multiple wins in the Masters Tournament, the British Open, and the U.S. Open, Jack Nicklaus had more than established himself among the golfing elite.

But in 1986, a forty-six-year-old Nicklaus was coming off two of the worst years of his career. In several tournaments, he had failed to even make the cut. When he did, he finished poorly, placing well behind the lead in five separate tournaments. For the first time in twenty-two years, Nicklaus failed to qualify for the U.S. Open. Even worse, shortly before the Masters, a golf magazine ranked Nicklaus 160th in terms of winnings. It wasn't that Nicklaus needed the income, but for a golfer of his stature, it was painfully embarrassing.

He turned to his friends for help. His longtime teacher Jack Grout watched Nicklaus play in the Doral Open and issued a pithy three-word diagnosis: "Way too handsy." Grout made his pupil practice the basics, insisting Nicklaus apply the mantra he had been taught in his youth: "Reach for the sky swinging back, and reach for it again swinging through." After practicing his swing and incorporating advice from fellow golfer Chi Chi Rodriguez about his pitching stance, Nicklaus was feeling better about his game than he had in years. And to make him even more comfortable, his son Jackie, a pro golfer himself, offered to caddy for his dad in the Masters.

In Nicklaus' first three rounds at the 1986 Masters, held in Augusta, Georgia, he shot rounds of seventy-four, seventy-one, and sixty-nine. Coming into the fourth and final round, he was two under par. There were four strokes and seven players between Nicklaus and the tournament leader, Greg Norman. Facing the press after shooting sixty-nine in the third round, a reporter asked him about the last time he had shot under seventy. Nicklaus thought for a minute, and replied that it was so long ago, he honestly couldn't remember.

On Sunday morning, the day of the last round, Nicklaus' second son, Steve, called him and asked what he thought it would take to win the tournament. Nicklaus told him he believed it would take a sixty-six to tie, and a sixty-five to win. Steve replied, "That's the number I've been thinking of. Go shoot it."

For the next few hours, Nicklaus turned back the clock. And as he walked from hole to hole, sinking birdie putts and playing some of the smartest golf of his life, the field came back to him. One by one his competitors faltered. And as Nicklaus rose in the ranks, the crowd response grew exponentially.

*(left to right) Jack Nicklaus watches his putt drop for a birdie on the 17th hole, giving him the lead in the Masters. ■ Nicklaus pitches out of a sandtrap to win the British Amateur Golf Championship. May 27, 1959*

The fans were smitten by the drama of this legend seemingly coming from out of the past to challenge the superstars of the present.

By the time Nicklaus was on the 17th tee, there was only one man left to beat. Seve Ballesteros was two holes behind him, and as Nicklaus stepped up to address his tee shot, the silence was broken by the roar of the crowd at the 15th hole. Ballesteros had just sunk his ball in the lake in front of the 15th green. Nicklaus birdied the 17th hole and took Ballesteros' place in the lead.

*(clockwise from upper left) Nicklaus hits out of the sand. ■ Nicklaus celebrates the round that would give him his sixth Masters victory. ■ As in the '86 Masters, Jack Nicklaus II, left, caddies for his father as the elder Nicklaus speaks with fellow golfer Arnold Palmer, right.*

With just the 18th hole to go, the old adage that golf is 10 percent physical and 90 percent mental proved itself true again. Nicklaus, who'd played aggressively the whole day, changed his strategy. In his book, *Jack Nicklaus: My Story*, he recalls telling himself, "You've had an incredible run to get where you are, so don't go and screw it up now by trying to cap yourself with a birdie at eighteen. Just go ahead and play the hole intelligently."

He reached the green of the par four hole in two strokes, and when he walked onto the green, he received an ovation worthy of a conquering hero. He described it as, "Deafening, stunning, unbelievable in every way. Tears kept coming to my eyes and I had to tell myself a number of times to hold back on the emotions, that I still had some golf to play." Jack putted twice, parring the hole, and now all that remained was to wait for the other contenders to finish. Greg Norman had the last good chance to tie or win. He had birdied fourteen through seventeen and if he parred eighteen, he'd tie Nicklaus. But as millions watched, Norman faltered, bogeying the last hole. Jack Nicklaus had done the unexpected, he'd come back to win his sixth Masters.

### Jack Nicklaus Victories

| | |
|---|---|
| **Masters Tournament** | **6** |
| **P.G.A. Championship** | **5** |
| **U.S. Open** | **4** |
| **British Open** | **3** |

**Plus, almost eighty other professional victories in the U.S. and abroad.**

*(top to bottom)
Nicklaus tries on the coveted green jacket for the third time. April 11, 1966 ■ 1985 Masters winner Bernhard Langer helps Nicklaus don the green jacket twenty-three years after he first won the tournament.*

"I don't believe what I just saw! One of the most remarkable finishes to any World Series game!"

Jack Buck

# Dodgers Win on Kirk Gibson Home Run

The Los Angeles Dodgers were not favored to win the 1988 World Series against the Oakland A's. Oakland boasted a strong pitching staff and a squad of home run threats. Dodgers outfielder Kirk Gibson turned out to be his team's best home run hitter, but in winning game seven of the National League Playoff Series against the New York Mets, he had injured his right knee. That pain only added to the ripped hamstring he'd been nursing in his left leg. When game one of the World Series started, Gibson was in no shape to play.

In the fifth inning, announcer Vin Scully broke the news that Gibson wouldn't be appearing that night. Gibson was watching the telecast while receiving physical therapy in the clubhouse. Inspired, he got off the trainer's bench and started hitting balls off a tee into a net. He then notified Dodgers manager Tommy Lasorda that he was available to bat if necessary.

Back under the lights at Dodger Stadium, the Dodgers were behind 4 to 3 in the bottom of the ninth inning. Oakland pitcher Dennis Eckersley, the best reliever in baseball, was on the mound. The Dodgers were down to their last out. With one man on base, Lasorda called for Gibson to pinch hit for the pitcher. Knowing Gibson's condition from media reports and from his pronounced limp on the way to the plate, the crowd welcomed him like a hero.

Gibson fouled off the first pitch and it was obvious from his swing that his legs were nearly useless. Eckersley threw his second pitch, and again Gibson fouled it off, but looked stronger. After Gibson took three balls and fouled off two more pitches, the count was full. The stadium's fifty-five thousand fans were on their feet.

Eckersley threw and Gibson swung and connected, sending a game-winning home run over the right field fence. Gibson triumphantly circled the bases, pumping his fist in the air as he hobbled to home plate. In the announcers' booth, Jack Buck, broadcasting over CBS Radio, was absolutely awestruck, stating with wonder, "Unbelievable!…Is this really happening? I don't believe what I just saw! One of the most remarkable finishes to any World Series game!"

Gibson would not bat again in the Series that year. But his incredible moment in game one was made even better when the Dodgers went on to become the 1988 World Champions in five games.

*(clockwise from left) Gibson rounds the bases after his home run. ■ Gibson hits the game-winning shot. ■ Gibson is mobbed by teammates after his home run.*

"The biggest upset in the history of heavyweight championship fights."
Jim Lampley

# Buster Douglas Upsets Mike Tyson

By age twenty-nine, James "Buster" Douglas had a respectable record as a heavyweight boxer with twenty-nine wins, four losses, and one draw, but he wasn't considered to be in the same class as heavyweight champion Mike Tyson.

In 1986, at the age of twenty, Tyson became the youngest boxer ever to win a heavyweight title when he scored a second-round knockout over Trevor Berbick to become the World Boxing Council champion. Over the next four years, Tyson proved to be the dominating force in heavyweight boxing with a record of thirty-seven wins, no losses, and thirty-three knockouts.

When Tyson was the champ, it wasn't a case of if he would win, it was how long his opponent would last and how savage the knockout would be. He knocked out previous champion Larry Holmes in four rounds, Michael Spinks in ninety-one seconds, and Carl Williams in ninety-three seconds. Because of his fighter's strength, Tyson's promoter, Don King, began to run out of big-name fighters for bouts. But he still needed to provide big paydays for his client, so he set his sights on Douglas. Boxing experts and oddsmakers, though, saw Douglas as little threat to Tyson and the heavyweight title.

On February 11, 1990, in Tokyo's Korakuen Stadium and broadcast live to the rest of the world as a pay-per-view event, Buster Douglas entered the ring against "Iron" Mike Tyson with long odds against him. Douglas announced his strategy before the match, saying, "I'll just hit him, I guess." And hit him he did.

Douglas came out strong in the first two rounds with a series of crisp rights. He was taller than Tyson, 6 feet 4 inches to 5 feet 11 inches, and his longer reach worked to his advantage. But perhaps more important was that Douglas didn't seem to fear Tyson. As the fight progressed, the underdog's confidence grew. Fans were stunned to see Tyson begin to falter under Douglas' heavy blows in the fifth round. Nobody had ever injured Tyson to such an extent before.

Douglas continued to dominate the fight, but late in the eighth round he got careless, and Tyson delivered a hard right uppercut that sent Douglas to the canvas. The knockdown timekeeper began his countdown as Douglas hit the floor, but the referee started his own count two seconds after the timekeeper. Douglas kept his eyes on the referee's hands for the count. He got up as the referee called

*(left to right) Tyson falls under Douglas' blows during the 10th and final round of their Tokyo title bout. ■ Tyson with promoter Don King in Las Vegas, June 1990*

the nine-count, but eleven seconds after the time-keeper began. Despite the apparent discrepancy, the fight continued.

Douglas came out punching in the ninth round, pounding away at Tyson and closing the champ's left eye completely. By the 10th round, Tyson could not see what was coming at him.

Midway into the 10th round, Douglas hit Tyson with an uppercut, then two more hard punches, sending Tyson's mouthpiece flying as his body hit the canvas. "Down goes Tyson!" declared Jim Lampley, the veteran sportscaster anchoring the telecast. As the referee began the count, Tyson struggled to get on all fours, searching for his mouth guard, and then clumsily regained his footing. Although Tyson rose on the nine-count, the referee bear hugged him and stopped the contest at 1:23 into the 10th round. Over the stunned roar of the crowd, Lampley shouted, "Mike Tyson has been knocked out! Unbelievable! Let's go ahead and call it—the biggest upset in the history of heavyweight championship fights!"

*(top to bottom) Douglas receives the count from the referee after Tyson knocked him down in the eighth round.* ■ *Douglas throws a right hook to Tyson's head in the first round.* ■ *Douglas continues to pummel the faltering heavyweight champion.*

Seeing his top fighter lose, promoter Don King immediately filed a protest based on the discrepancy of the eighth-round count between the referee and the timekeeper. King believed Douglas had been knocked out, but his protest was overruled and Douglas was declared boxing's new heavyweight champion.

Douglas' first title defense after beating Tyson came against 1984 Olympic bronze medalist boxer Evander Holyfield in October 1990. Holyfield knocked Douglas out in the third round, and by doing so, knocked Douglas out of the boxing spotlight. Still, for one night in February 1990, James "Buster" Douglas stood alone, owning one of the greatest sporting titles on earth, the heavyweight championship of the world.

(top to bottom) Tyson falls after Douglas lands the knockout punch that earned him the heavyweight title. ■ Douglas celebrates after ending Tyson's four-year reign as heavyweight champion.

"Carl Lewis...blazing to the finish for the U.S! What about the world record? Yes! Yes!"
**Tom Hammond**

# Carl Lewis Anchors U.S. Olympic Victory

**C**arl Lewis' record places him at the very pinnacle of Olympic achievement. In four Olympics, he won a total of nine gold medals, matching Paavo Nurmi, the Finnish runner who collected his ninth gold medal at the 1928 Olympics, and Soviet gymnast Larissa Latynina, who earned her ninth gold medal in 1964.

Lewis won his first four gold medals at the 1984 Los Angeles Olympics, capturing first place in the long jump, the 100 meters, and the 200 meters. He captured his fourth medal anchoring the American team in the 4 x 100 relay. That team not only won the gold medal, but also broke the world record with a time of 37.83.

Four years later, in Seoul, Korea, Lewis won gold in his second consecutive long jump. He then was awarded the gold in the 100 meters by default when the original winner, Canadian sprinter Ben Johnson, tested positive for steroids and was stripped of his medal.

At the 1992 Olympics, held in Barcelona, Spain, Lewis flew to his third consecutive long jump win and his seventh gold medal. His only other shot at a medal was in the 4 x 100-meter relay, and that came only on a fluke. It hadn't been a great year for Lewis. Before the Olympic trials, he'd contracted a sinus infection that had spread to his thyroid, liver, and kidneys, and he was nowhere near his best. For the first time, he'd failed to qualify for either the 100- or 200-meter sprints. When the Games started, he wasn't even one of the four runners on the 4 x 100 squad, but had qualified as an alternate.

But in the 100-meter semifinals, U.S. relay member Mark Witherspoon ruptured his Achilles tendon and Lewis was called upon to anchor the 4 x 100 for a third straight Olympics. The fact that he was competing in just two events might have been detrimental to his overall medal count, but it was advantageous for the American team. The thirty-one-year-old Lewis had more time to rest between heats. And when it came time for the final, the rest paid off.

That day, when Lewis took his place on the track, he'd already anchored five world record relay teams. In addition, he'd run fourteen 100-meter races in under ten seconds, and long jumped twenty-eight

*(left to right) Lewis crosses the finish line of the 1992 relay. Nigeria's Davidson Ezinwa, left, and Cuba's Jorge Luis Aguilera Ruiz, right, celebrate their teams' second- and third-place finishes. ■ Members of the U.S. and Jamaican teams raise Lewis on their shoulders after Lewis won his fourth gold.*

(left to right) Lewis sprints to victory in the anchor leg of the 4 x 100 relay team in the 1984 Summer Olympics. ■ Canadian Ben Johnson, in foreground, and Lewis race in the 1988 Olympics. Lewis received the gold medal in the 100 meters when Johnson was disqualified.

feet or more sixty times. He had nothing to prove. But, in many people's minds, it would be his most stunning performance.

By the time Michael Marsh and Leroy Burrell had completed their legs, and Dennis Mitchell slapped the baton into Lewis' outstretched palm for the final one hundred meters, the American runners were one meter ahead of the second-place team from Nigeria. But the moment he received the baton, a fire was lit. Lewis' face broke into a grin, he took his first five strides with the baton, and yelled, "Yes!" once, then, "Yes!" again and kicked his long legs into overdrive.

In that last leg, Lewis stretched that one-meter lead to seven meters—from three feet to more than twenty. As the official time flashed on the scoreboard, the crowd and Lewis began to celebrate. The American team had set another world record, shaving a tenth of a second off the old record and finishing in 37.40. Lewis had just possibly run the fastest running-start one hundred meters of his life—a startling 8.8 seconds.

Four years later, a graying thirty-five-year-old Lewis would cap off his amazing career at the 1996 Olympic Games in Atlanta by winning a fourth consecutive long jump and ninth Olympic gold medal. With that victory, he not only tied for the most gold medals won by a single athlete, but joined American discus thrower Al Oerter as the only competitors ever to win the same event in four consecutive Olympic Games.

*(clockwise from lower left) Lewis flies to a long jump gold medal in the 1992 Olympics.* ■ *Lewis celebrates his first-place finish in the 1992 4 x 100 relay while Nigeria's Ezinwa signifies his placement.* ■ *Members of the 1992 4 x 100 relay team. From left: Michael Marsh, Leroy Burrell, Dennis Mitchell, Carl Lewis.* ■ *At the 1996 Centennial Olympics, Lewis receives his ninth gold medal.*

> "Wayne Gretzky's NHL record book is now complete."
>
> Bob Miller

# Wayne Gretzky
# Captures NHL Scoring Mark

It began in a backyard hockey rink at 42 Varadi Avenue in Brantford, Ontario. The neighborhood kids called the rink "Wally Coliseum" after the owner of the house, Walter Gretzky. Walter would flood his backyard each winter, turning the lawn into a hockey rink for his five children. All the Gretzky children were good athletes, but Wayne, the oldest of four brothers, seemed to excel at hockey at a very early age.

Wayne Gretzky learned to skate at age two. When he was six years old, he played in a league for ten-year-olds. In fact, all through his youth hockey career, he played with kids who were two, three, and four years older, and at each step, he was the best player on the ice.

When Gretzky was nine, he scored 196 goals and added 120 assists in a seventy-six-game season. Soon, media attention started to focus on the young hockey phenom. Playing off his last name, a member of the local media nicknamed the nine-year-old, "The Great Gretzky," a name he proudly shouldered for his entire career.

Gretzky was invariably the smallest on his team, since he was always playing on teams with older kids. With his father's help, he learned to modify the fit of his always-too-big team uniforms. Walter had Wayne tuck in the right side of his jersey so he could shoot the puck without getting his stick caught in his clothing. Gretzky stuck with the "tuck" throughout his NHL career, always tucking the right half of his jersey into his pants.

By the time Gretzky was seventeen, he was ready for professional hockey, but the National Hockey League would not sign players until they had graduated from Junior A hockey. Because the rival World Hockey Association needed players to keep their struggling league alive, the WHA's Indianapolis Racers signed the young superstar from Ontario.

Wayne Gretzky's career in Indianapolis lasted a total of eight games. Indianapolis was not a hockey town and without fan or financial support, the owner traded Gretzky to the WHA Edmonton Oilers. The next season, the NHL absorbed the WHA and with it came the Oilers and the team's star player, Gretzky.

Gretzky became an immediate NHL success. In his first season, he won the first of eight consecutive Hart Trophies, awarded to the league's most valuable player. With a collection of players like

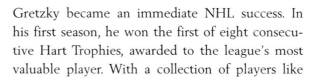

*(clockwise from left) Gretzky celebrates after scoring his 802$^{nd}$ goal. ■ Thirteen-year-old Gretzky in 1972 ■ Gretzky raises the Stanley Cup over his head after the Oilers defeated the New York Islanders. May 19, 1984*

*Gretzky scores his 801st goal to tie Gordie Howe's career scoring record. March 20, 1994*

in their prime, it appeared the Oilers dynasty would not end.

By the summer of 1988, Oilers owner Peter Pocklington was in financial trouble. To save his team, he sacrificed his most valuable and marketable asset. On August 9, 1988, Pocklington traded Gretzky to the Los Angeles Kings in a lucrative multi-player deal that earned Pocklington $15 million dollars.

By this time in his career, Gretzky owned all of the single-season scoring records. He now had two tasks: make Los Angeles into a hockey town, and break his boyhood idol Gordie Howe's career scoring records.

Gretzky, Mark Messier, Jari Kurri, Glenn Anderson, Paul Coffey, and Grant Fuhr, the Oilers started to pile up wins, and Gretzky piled up points.

In 1980, Gretzky began his amazing string of seven straight league scoring titles. But he didn't just win individual titles, he set records, or more correctly, he smashed them. In 1981, he broke the NHL's single-season scoring record with 164 points (55 goals and 109 assists). In 1982, he shattered Phil Esposito's 1971 single-season goal-scoring record of seventy-six goals by scoring ninety-two in the 1981-82 season. That season stands out because Gretzky scored 212 points—the first of his four two hundred-plus-point seasons. Nobody was even close to Gretzky in scoring, and with Gretzky leading the way, the Edmonton Oilers won four Stanley Cups in five years. With so many great players

Night after night, Gretzky played before sell-out crowds in Los Angeles, and night after night he got closer to Howe's career marks of 1,850 points and 801 goals. On October 15, 1989, appropriately against the Oilers in Edmonton, the first of Howe's records fell. With fifty-three seconds left in the third period, and Howe watching in the stands, Gretzky scored for the Kings to tie the game. It was Gretzky's 1,851st point. He then scored in overtime to give the Kings the victory. On his broken record, Howe said, "I kissed that record good-bye a long time ago when Wayne started getting two hundred points a year."

There was just one more record to break, 801 goals, and this time it happened in Los Angeles in front of the home crowd. On March 23, 1994, against the Vancouver Canucks, at 14:47 into the

second period, "The Great Gretzky" became the greatest goal scorer of all time with his 802nd career goal. Kings play-by-play announcer Bob Miller forever etched the moment in fans' minds as he described the record goal: "Wayne Gretzky's NHL record book is now complete. He's the all-time leader in points, assists, and now with his 802nd goal, the all-time leading goal scorer in the history of the National Hockey League!"

## Wayne Gretzky's Career Statistics

| | |
|---|---|
| **Highest Single-Season** | |
| **Points Scored (1985-86)** | **215** |
| **Career Goals** | **894** |
| **Career Assists** | **1,963** |
| **Total Points Scored** | **2,857** |

In 1996, Wayne Gretzky was traded to the St. Louis Blues, where he would spend half a year before signing with the New York Rangers for his final three seasons. He played his last NHL game with the Rangers on April 18, 1999, and scored his final point, an assist. In a ceremony before the game, the NHL retired Gretzky's famous No. 99 forever in honor of his contributions to the sport of hockey. When it was all over, "The Great Gretzky" owned an unprecedented sixty-one NHL scoring records, including the most career goals with 894, and the most assists with 1,963, for a grand total of 2,857 points scored.

*(upper left) Gretzky breaks Howe's record with his 802nd goal. ■ (right) Following his final game, Gretzky is applauded by teammates as he waves good-bye to his fans.*

"Well, New York. After
fifty-four years, your
long wait is over."

Gary Bettman

# New York Rangers Win Stanley Cup

The New York Rangers won hockey's top prize, the Stanley Cup, in 1940. But during the next half-century, the team came up empty-handed year after year.

Fans' luck started to change in the early 1990s when the Rangers started to put together a team worthy of challenging for the Cup. Most notably they acquired center Mark Messier, who had previously won five Stanley Cups with the Edmonton Oilers. In April 1993, they hired Mike Keenan as their head coach. Keenan had previously taken the Philadelphia Flyers to two Stanley Cup finals and the Chicago Blackhawks to one, but lost all three times. Keenan had a volatile temper and was not popular with the players or Rangers general manager Neil Smith, but he had a sense of purpose and a dedication to winning the Stanley Cup.

During the 1993-94 regular season, the Rangers played well, finishing with a record of 52-24-8, the best record in the National Hockey League.

The Rangers started the Stanley Cup playoffs with two series victories, sweeping the New York Islanders in four games and beating the Washington Capitals 4 games to 1. In the semifinal series with the New Jersey Devils, the Rangers took an early 2 games to 1 lead going into game four at New Jersey. During game four, though, coach Keenan's temper got the best of him and he benched several

players and limited the playing time of others, including goaltender Mike Richter, defenseman Brian Leetch, and captain Mark Messier. The Rangers lost the game and the series was tied at two. Turmoil surrounded the players and their coach. Keenan apologized to the team before game five, but the Rangers had already lost their focus. The Devils won the game and the Rangers were one game away from elimination. Messier made a bold prediction. He guaranteed a victory in game six against the Devils and he delivered it almost single-handedly.

The Rangers were down 2 to 1 going into the third period when Messier scored three consecutive goals, a natural "hat trick." The Rangers won 4 to 2, setting up game seven, with the winner advancing to the Stanley Cup finals.

In game seven, the Rangers led 1 to 0 until the final seconds when the Devils' Valeri Zelepukin scored with 7.7 seconds left in regulation. The tie extended

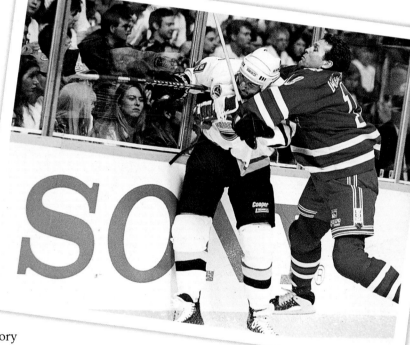

*(left to right) Rangers goalie Mike Richter makes a save in the third period of the final game against the Canucks.*
■ *New York's Craig MacTavish checks Vancouver's Tim Hunter.*

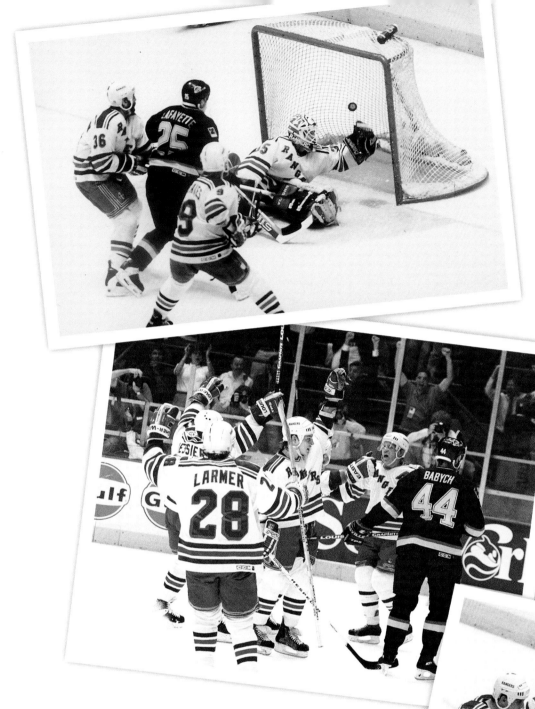

the game into overtime, then double overtime, before the Rangers' Stephane Matteau scored the game-winning goal.

The Rangers met the Vancouver Canucks in the Stanley Cup finals and established a sizable series lead—3 games to 1. Just one game away from a New York championship, news reports circulated that Keenan had agreed to become the coach and general manager of the Detroit Red Wings after the season. The rumors distracted the Rangers, and they lost the next two games, taking the series into a winner-take-all game seven.

In his pregame speech, Keenan admitted his mistakes to his team, conceding that he was too demanding but imploring them to earn the championship. Messier later called it one of the most inspirational speeches he had ever heard. The Rangers responded well, taking a 2 to 0 lead by the end of the first period. In the second period, the Canucks posted their first goal when they slapped one past Rangers goaltender Mike Richter, putting the score at 2 to 1. But at 13:29 of the second period, Messier scored to give the Rangers a 3 to 1 lead.

*(top to bottom) Vancouver threatens in the third period, but New York goalie Mike Richter does not let them score. ■ Brian Leech (wearing face guard) and teammates celebrate his first-period goal. ■ The Rangers crowd the ice to celebrate after winning their first Stanley Cup in fifty-four years.*

The final period was a high-pressure affair. The Canucks' Trevor Linden scored at 4:50 in the third period to tighten the Rangers' lead to just one goal. Vancouver continued to threaten, but the Rangers played tough defense the last fifteen minutes of the game. In the final gut-wrenching ninety seconds, there were four faceoffs in the Rangers' end of the ice, the last with 1.6 seconds remaining. Craig MacTavish won it for the Rangers, knocking the puck to the boards where it was smothered, and the Rangers had won their first Stanley Cup in fifty-four years.

After seven minutes of wild celebration on the ice and in the stands of New York's Madison Square Garden, NHL Commissioner Gary Bettman came out on the ice and said over the loudspeaker, "Well, New York. After fifty-four years, your long wait is over. Mark Messier, come get the Stanley Cup." With that, Messier and the Rangers skated around the ice with the Cup hoisted above their heads, sharing it with fans who had gone generations without hockey's most coveted trophy.

*(top to bottom) Coach Mike Keenan and the New York Rangers ■ Rangers captain Mark Messier shows off the Stanley Cup in a postgame celebration.*

"A win for the ages."

Jim Nantz

# Tiger Woods Wins Masters

Eldrick "Tiger" Woods is a true phenomenon, a genuine golf prodigy who first showed his affinity for the game before he could walk. He is also a young minority participating in an arena long dominated by white players. And in the spring of 1997, he captured America's heart when he strode triumphantly up the 18th fairway at the Augusta National Golf Club, hugged his dad, and slipped on the coveted green jacket given to the winner of the Masters, one of golf's most prestigious tournaments.

The Woods legend began at age two, when Tiger was introduced to a national audience. He appeared on the "Mike Douglas Show" and swapped putts with Bob Hope. At the age of three, he shot a forty-eight for nine holes. His father and teacher, Earl, says that at six months, his baby boy was watching him hit golf balls into a net, and soon after, the little tyke imitated his daddy's swing.

By the time Woods was sixteen, he'd won countless trophies, including six Optimist International Junior tournaments, the Insurance Youth Golf Classic (the youngest ever to win it), and before he graduated to the U.S. Amateur tournament, he won the Junior Amateur three years running. In 1994, he won the first of his three consecutive U.S. Amateurs, the first player ever to do so. As a student-athlete at Stanford, he won the NCAA championship and was named Collegiate Player of the Year.

Just after turning professional in summer 1996, a twenty-year-old Woods won two PGA tournaments, the Las Vegas Invitational and the Walt Disney World/Oldsmobile Classic. The Mercedes Championship kicked off the 1997 PGA Tour in January, and Woods got off to a flying start by beating tour veteran Tom Lehman with a playoff-round birdie. In February, he crossed the Pacific and won the Asian Honda Classic by ten strokes. Then came the 1997 Masters Tournament.

The Masters is a tournament rich in heritage that dates back to 1934, and is the only major tournament that's played every year at the same exclusive course in Augusta, Georgia. Until early in the 1990s, the club had not integrated its membership, allowing only whites to join. This, of course, added a compelling spin to Woods' story.

After starting the first nine holes of the tournament slowly, Woods served notice on the back nine, shooting a red-hot thirty—six strokes under par. By the end of the second round, he took the lead for good with a sixty-six, surpassing that the next day with a third-round tally of sixty-five.

*(left to right) Woods hits his ball out of a bunker on the fifth hole of the final round of the 1997 Masters. ■ Woods contemplates his putt on the sixth green during the final round of the 1997 Masters.*

*Woods celebrates his record-breaking performance at the 1997 Masters.*

To the general public and the gallery at Augusta, the Masters had become the Tiger Woods Show. Going into the fourth and final round, it wasn't a question of whether Tiger Woods would win, but by how many strokes, and how many records would fall in the process.

In the final round, Woods reached the tee at the 18th and final hole with several records nearly assured. But he still needed a par to beat perhaps

the most regarded record, the four-round Masters score of 271, a mark held by legends Jack Nicklaus and Raymond Floyd. A par would put Woods in the clubhouse at 270.

Woods hooked his tee shot well left of the fairway at eighteen. He quickly regained his composure with his second shot, a high-arching wedge which placed his ball on the green. Nonetheless, a two-putt on the greens of Augusta is never a certainty, and the gallery waited with anticipation.

Woods' first putt left him within four feet of the hole. Although the fairways at Augusta echoed with the incredible ovation Woods received as he approached the green, the gallery was silent as he drew back the putter for his second putt. The ball sank into the cup, Woods triumphantly pumped his fist, and the crowd exploded into a roar. "A win for the ages," declared CBS commentator Jim Nantz as the ball dropped in the hole.

Tiger Woods finished his four rounds at the 1997 Masters with an eighteen-strokes-under-par 270, topping the mark held by Nicklaus and Floyd. The victory was also a Masters-record twelve strokes over second-place finisher Tom Kite, the largest winning margin in a major tournament in more than 125 years. Plus, at twenty-one years, three months, and fourteen days, Woods was the youngest golfer ever to win the green jacket—the traditional "trophy" bestowed to the Masters champion. He was also the first African American, and the first Asian, ever to win the sixty-three-year-old event.

As Woods walked up the slope to the scorer's tent behind the 18th green, he spotted his father, who only the month before had undergone bypass heart surgery. Tiger hugged him and tears streamed down both their faces. The kid who'd copied his dad's swing in his crib just two decades before, had finally arrived, and so had the next chapter in professional golf history.

*(left to right) Woods embraces his caddy, Mike Cowan, after his Masters victory. ■ 1996 Masters champion Nick Faldo helps Woods don the traditional green jacket. ■ Woods displays the Masters trophy.*

"If that's the last image of Michael Jordan, how magnificent is it?"

Bob Costas

# Michael Jordan Wins Sixth NBA Championship

He seemed to defy gravity by staying up in the air longer than the other players. He had an uncanny way of shooting on the way down from his jump shot, after his defender was already on the floor. He could do it all: handle the ball, pass, shoot outside, score inside, rebound, and play defense.

But it wasn't always that way for Michael Jordan, who was cut from his high school basketball team in Wilmington, North Carolina, as a sophomore. He returned his junior year, however, to begin the career that would make him a worldwide icon.

He took his talents to the University of North Carolina to play for coach Dean Smith. It was there that basketball scouts began to notice Jordan. As a freshman at North Carolina, he hit the game-winning shot in the 1982 NCAA championship game to give North Carolina a 63 to 62 win over Georgetown and its star player, Patrick Ewing.

After his junior season, Jordan left North Carolina, where he won the Naismith and Wooden Awards as college basketball's top player. He was picked third overall in the NBA draft by the Chicago Bulls, behind Hakeem Olajuwon, who went to Houston, and Sam Bowie, who went to Portland. In his first year, Jordan averaged 28.2 points per game, helped take the Bulls to the playoffs, and was voted both an All-Star Game starter and the NBA Rookie of the Year.

In 1987, Jordan won the first of seven straight NBA scoring titles. But aside from his scoring talent, perhaps Jordan's most notable traits were his unselfish play and his ability to lead. With Jordan on the floor, other players found their roles and were allowed to shine. The Bulls began assembling a cast of players, including Scottie Pippen, Horace Grant, and Bill Cartwright, who would complement him and make up the core of a team that would become an NBA force.

Though it took Jordan seven seasons in the NBA before the Bulls won their first title, once they had a championship, they were unstoppable. Chicago beat the Los Angeles Lakers in five games to capture the championship in 1991, then defeated the Portland Trail Blazers and the Phoenix Suns for the title the next two seasons. Jordan proved to be a dominant player in clutch games. He was named finals MVP each championship year and averaged an NBA Finals record forty-one points per game against the Suns.

*(left to right) With millions watching and the championship on the line, Jordan hits the game-winning shot in the 1998 NBA Finals. ■ Jordan as an NBA rookie in 1984*

*(clockwise from top left) Georgetown put heavy defense on Jordan when he had possession in the 1982 NCAA championship game. ■ Despite pressure from Patrick Ewing, Jordan sets to take a shot. ■ With only seventeen seconds left and his team down by one point, Jordan shoots the game-winning shot for North Carolina while Ewing (33) looks on.*

But then, on October 6, 1993, Jordan stunned basketball fans worldwide, announcing his retirement from the NBA. He wanted to give baseball a try, and spent the 1994 season playing for the Class AA Birmingham Barons, a Chicago White Sox farm team. He became the best-known minor league outfielder in America, but for his talent on the basketball court, not the baseball diamond. Jordan played respectably, hitting .259 in his last month of baseball, with fifty RBIs and thirty stolen bases overall. Though he was improving, Jordan left the ballpark for good when a players' strike canceled the World Series and lingered into 1995.

With a simple two-word fax to the media proclaiming, "I'm back," Jordan returned to basketball and Chicago mid-season in 1995. Only slightly rusty and temporarily wearing jersey number 45, he led the Bulls to a 13-4 record over the final seventeen games of the regular season. His performances included a remarkable fifty-five point outing in a victory over the New York Knicks just nine days after his first game back. But with the team still out of sync after Jordan's return, Chicago lost to Orlando in the second round of the playoffs. It would be the last time the Bulls would lose a playoff series with Jordan in the lineup.

In the 1995-96 season, Jordan's first full season back from baseball, the Bulls posted a 72-10 record, the best in NBA history. Jordan recaptured the scoring title and the team capped the season with its fourth championship. Again in 1996-97, Jordan

*(clockwise from left) Jordan slam dunks.* ■ *Jordan embraces his father, James, following the Bulls victory in the 1992 NBA Finals.* ■ *Following his retirement from basketball, Jordan spent the 1994 season playing for the Birmingham Barons.*

won the scoring title, and the Bulls won the championship. The 1997-98 season brought Jordan the scoring title for a record 10th time, and once more the Bulls found themselves in the finals.

In a rematch of the previous year, the opponents were the Utah Jazz, led by Karl Malone and John Stockton. The Bulls were led by a team that had been together for two years: Michael Jordan, Scottie Pippen, Dennis Rodman, Tony Kukoc, Steve Kerr, and coach Phil Jackson.

The 1998 championship series began in Utah. In game one, Stockton's twenty-four points and eight assists were enough to eke out an 88 to 85 over-time victory for the Jazz. But the series was evened in game two, when the Bulls took advantage of Karl Malone's failure to score in the second half, ending the game 93 to 88. The Bulls took game three in a home-court 96 to 54 blowout, with Utah posting the fewest points in any NBA game since the addi-

*(top to bottom) Utah's Shandon Anderson plays defense against Jordan in game six of the 1998 finals. ■ Jordan dribbles past Utah's Bryon Russell in game five of the 1997 finals. ■ Jordan goes up for a shot during game five of the 1998 finals.*

 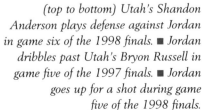

tion of the twenty-four-second shot clock. Rod-man's rebounding helped bring another Bulls win in a close game four, with a score of 86 to 82. Malone's thirty-nine points in game five overpowered the Bulls in an 83 to 81 victory.

Chicago now led the series 3 games to 2. A win for the Bulls at the Delta Center in Salt Lake City would clinch Chicago's sixth NBA title in eight years. The Bulls trailed the Jazz by three points in the final minute. Jordan scored on a drive to cut the Utah lead to one. The Jazz brought the ball up the court and put the ball in the hands of Karl Malone, who lost the ball to Jordan on the defensive end of the court.

With less than ten seconds remaining, Jordan had the ball near the top of the key. Guarded by Bryon Russell, Jordan faked in, Russell took the fake, and Jordan stuck a twenty-foot fade-away jumper in the basket with 5.2 seconds left on the clock to give the Bulls an 87 to 86 victory and a sixth NBA title. The game-winning jumper gave Jordan a total of forty-five points for the game and would be the final basket of his NBA career. In the end, Michael Jordan was able to fulfill the dream of most professional athletes, to go out on his own terms, to go out with dignity, and to go out on top.

(top to bottom) Jordan takes the last shot of the 1998 NBA Finals, and of his career. ■ Jordan and Bulls coach Phil Jackson show off the MVP and championship trophies, respectively, following Chicago's victory in the 1998 NBA Finals.

### Michael Jordan's Career Statistics

| | |
|---|---|
| NBA Scoring Titles | 10 |
| Career Scoring Average (points per game) | 31.5 |
| NBA MVP | 5 |
| All-Star Games | 11 |
| All-Star MVP | 3 |
| NBA Finals MVP | 6 |
| Olympic Gold Medals | 2 |

**"** It's all that we expected. It's incredible. There are no words. **"**

**Zinedine Zidane**

# France Wins World Cup on Home Soil

The World Cup was the invention of a Frenchman named Jules Rimet in 1930. Frenchman Lucien Laurent scored the very first goal in World Cup history in the first match on July 13, 1930. But nearly seventy years later, the French had yet to emerge victorious in what had become one of the grandest athletic competitions in the world.

In front of a capacity crowd on July 12, 1998, France played host country to the World Cup championship. The 64th and final game of the tournament pitted the defending champions, Brazil, against France, a decided underdog. Brazil was hoping for a fifth title win, having won in 1958, 1962, 1970, and 1994. This was the first appearance for Team France since its World Cup showing in 1986, when it beat Brazil in the quarterfinals, but then lost to West Germany in the semifinal round.

Team Brazil was formidable with its roster of superstar players, including midfielders Rivaldo and Denilson, fullback Roberto Carlos, goalkeeper Claudio Taffarel, and Brazil's best player, two-time FIFA World Player of the Year, striker Ronaldo.

Team France included world-class players, such as midfielder Emmanuel Petit and goalkeeper Fabien Barthez, defensive pillars Marcel Desailly and Lilian Thuram, and France's best playmaker, Zinedine Zidane.

Brazil was a no-show for the pre-match warm-up. Just hours before the game, superstar player Ronaldo fell ill, but later was cleared to play. After the game, Brazil's coach Mario Zagallo conceded that Ronaldo never should have played, but he was concerned about the possible effect the star's absence might have on the rest of the team.

France played aggressively from the opening kickoff. After just twenty-seven minutes, they were the first to score when Brazil's Carlos kicked the ball out-of-bounds along the end-line, allowing France a corner kick. As the kick arched to the goal, France's midfielder Zidane made it past Brazil's defenders and headed the ball past goalkeeper Taffarel.

The usually dominant Brazil team appeared to play cautiously while France seemed to thrive on the pressure. Before the end of the first half, France scored again on a corner kick from Youri Djorkaeff

*(left to right) France's goalkeeper Fabien Barthez leaps over Brazil's Ronaldo.* ■ *Emmanuel Petit boots the ball past Brazil's goalkeeper Claudio Taffarel in the final minutes.*

to Zidane, who again headed it into the net, this time between Carlos' legs. The score stood at 2 to 0, France. Zidane, known as the Magician of Marseille for his remarkable ball-handling skills, became the first player to score twice in a World Cup final since Argentina's Mario Kempes in the 1978 championship.

Brazil continued to play its slow pace, even under France's assault. Brazil's only real challenge came in the second half, when France's goalkeeper Fabien Barthez deflected a direct kick fired by Ronaldo from only eight meters in front of the net.

Despite their lead, France's midfielder Emmanual Petit relentlessly ran the field. In the game's final minutes, Petit and teammate, substitute midfielder Patrick Vieira, raced downfield, passing the ball back and forth toward Brazil's goal where Petit booted the ball into the corner of the net. The score was a stunning 3 to 0. Once the clock ticked off the final seconds, France erupted into a wild celebration, having

*(top to bottom) Zidane, far left, scores for France by heading the ball into the net off a corner kick.* ■ *The ball hits the net after Zidane (10) headed it past goalkeeper Taffarel.* ■ *Teammates congratulate Zidane after a goal.*

*(top to bottom) French President Jacques Chirac celebrates his country's World Cup victory.* ■ *Team France joins together after the medals ceremony.* ■ *France's captain Didier Deschamps raises the World Cup while teammates and fans celebrate.*

won its first World Cup. More than one million fans celebrated in the streets of Paris that evening.

"It's all that we expected. It's incredible. There are no words," Zidane said with tears and sweat streaming down his face. Brazilian coach Zagallo and the rest of his team were stunned. "Brazil lost the final in the first half," Zagallo conceded. "In the second half we did everything we could but we were not able to make up the difference....France was better."

**"Down the left
field line,
is it enough?
There it is,
sixty-two!"**

Joe Buck

# Mark McGwire Smashes Home Run Record

From the first day of the 1998 baseball season, there was excitement in the air. In that game, the St. Louis Cardinals big first baseman, thirty-four-year-old Mark McGwire, hit a towering grand slam home run. To follow, he hit home runs in each of his next three games, matching Willie Mays' National League record of homering in the season's first four games. The season was less than a week old and there was talk of records falling—sports fans were already predicting that McGwire, the Seattle Mariners' Ken Griffey Jr., or the Chicago White Sox's Albert Belle would eclipse Roger Maris' thirty-seven-year-old record of sixty-one home runs in a season.

By June, a new name catapulted into the home run race. The Chicago Cubs Dominican outfielder Sammy Sosa hit thirteen homers by the end of May, and another twenty in June. That performance set the record for home runs in a single month. By July, Sosa had a total of thirty-three home runs, just four behind McGwire. And just as Mickey Mantle had pushed Roger Maris in 1961, Sosa pushed McGwire.

The home run derby was on and the nation was watching. As other contenders faded, attention focused even further on McGwire and Sosa. Newspapers around the country began a record watch, with each player's total prominently set in its own box in the sports section every day.

Unlike the animosity Roger Maris faced from Babe Ruth fans and the media in 1961, McGwire and Sosa had the whole country on their side. The two had become American icons. McGwire was Paul Bunyan in a baseball uniform—a former Olympic athlete from a middle-class California family; a divorced father who remained good friends with his ex-wife. Sosa grew up in the Dominican Republic with a baseball glove made out of a milk carton; a successful twenty-nine-year-old immigrant who made it to the majors, proof that the American dream can come true. He was an inspiration for kids everywhere.

By the end of August, the question of whether one of baseball's most hallowed and respected records would be broken was not "if" but "by whom?" At midnight on August 31, McGwire and Sosa were tied at fifty-five home runs apiece.

*(clockwise from left) McGwire belts his record-breaking 62$^{nd}$ home run. ■ Roger Maris hits sixty-one in 1961. ■ Babe Ruth hits sixty in 1927.*

On September 1 and 2, McGwire's bat thundered against the Florida Marlins, hitting two home runs in each of two games, and breaking his own personal record of fifty-eight. Three days later, on September 5, he homered off Cincinnati's Dennis Reyes to tie Babe Ruth with sixty.

Two days later, in St. Louis' Busch Stadium, the drama was reaching its peak as the Cardinals began a two-game homestand against the Chicago Cubs and Sosa. There wasn't long to wait—in his first at-bat, McGwire took a 1-1 pitch from Mike Morgan and launched it over the left field fence, a 430-foot blast. McGwire had hit his 61$^{st}$ home run and tied Maris' record on his father's 61$^{st}$ birthday.

The next night, September 8, McGwire put an end to the race to break the record. In the fourth inning, he reached out and pushed a Steve Trachsel pitch just over the left field fence—ironically, his shortest home run of the season. But distance did not matter because this was number sixty-two, the home run that made history.

The crowd went wild and fireworks exploded. An exultant McGwire hopped, jumped, and loped around the bases, actually missing first base in the process and returning to tag it. After he touched home plate, he picked up his ten-year-old son, Matt, dressed in a kid-sized version of his father's

*McGwire hits his 62$^{nd}$, and shortest, home run of the 1998 season.*

*(opposite page, top to bottom) Sammy Sosa congratulates McGwire after his record-breaking home run. ■ McGwire went into the stands to hug Richard Maris after hitting the home run that broke his father's thirty-seven-year-old record. ■ McGwire lifts up his son at home plate.*

uniform, and hugged and kissed him. In his own show of sportsmanship, Sosa ran in from right field and embraced McGwire.

In a show of respect, McGwire went into the crowded stands and shook hands with and hugged each of Roger Maris' children. At the same moment he took their father's record, he honored it, and proved himself worthy.

Mark McGwire ended the season by establishing a new single-season record of seventy home runs, just four ahead of Sosa. Numerically, McGwire and Sosa had merely broken a longtime record. But in a larger sense, their run for the record captured America's imagination, helping restore the game of baseball to its role as America's pastime.

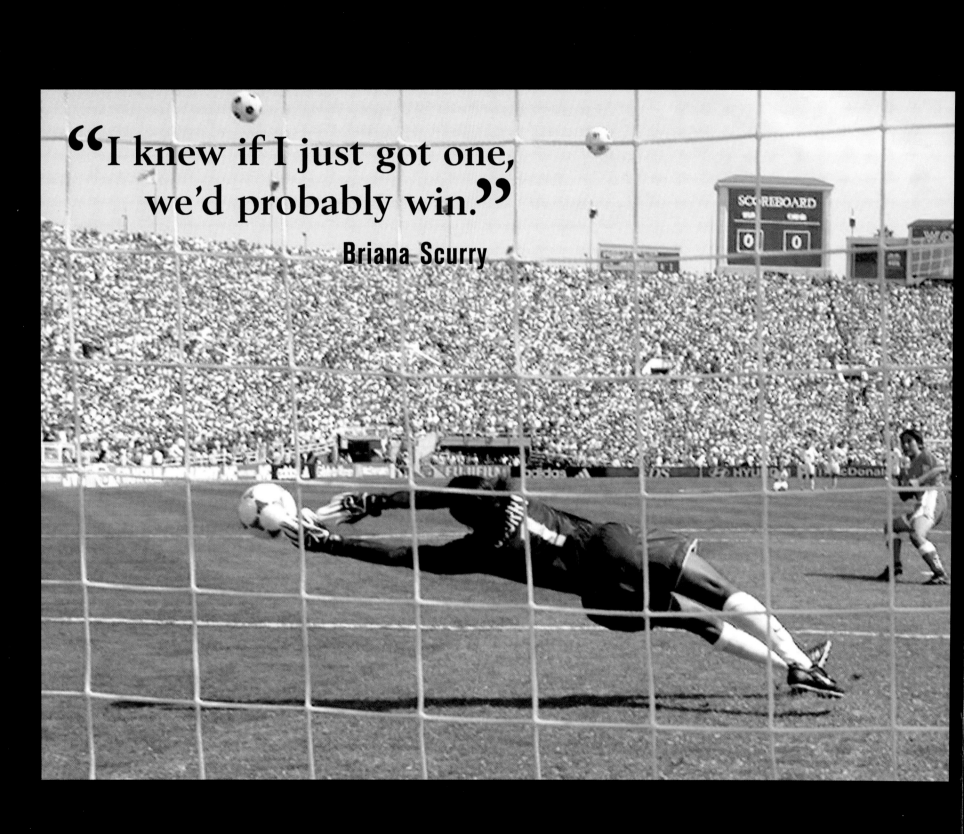

"I knew if I just got one, we'd probably win." Briana Scurry

# U.S. Women Win World Cup Soccer

The biggest sports event of summer 1999 was not hockey's Stanley Cup finals or even basketball's NBA championships. Television ratings show more people, an estimated forty million, glued their eyes on the United States versus China in women's World Cup soccer.

Though the game would go scoreless through regulation and two overtimes, the determination and defensive strategies of both teams kept viewers on the edges of their seats. The largest crowd in women's sports history—90,185 fans at the Rose Bowl in Pasadena, California—only added to the intensity.

As anticipated in pregame reports, the oldest member of the U.S. team, thirty-three-year-old midfielder Michelle Akers, anchored her team's defense. Known as one of the game's premiere blockers, she headed off China's advances by throwing herself at every airborne ball. But the Chinese caught a break when Akers collided with U.S. goalkeeper Briana Scurry near the end of regulation play and left the game.

China took advantage of Akers' departure. During ninety minutes of regulation play, the Chinese managed only two shots on the American net. With Akers gone, China took three shots in thirty minutes of sudden-death overtime—one of which almost sent U.S. fans home heartbroken.

Ten minutes into the first overtime, China midfielder Liu Ying directed a corner kick to teammate Fan Yunji, who headed the ball directly toward the left corner of the net. The ball soared past Scurry, but U.S. midfielder Kristine Lilly was in position just inside the goalpost. She headed the ball away from the net, saving the U.S. from certain defeat.

On went the remainder of the two fifteen-minute overtimes, with both teams hurling themselves from goal to goal, executing the defensive strategies that kept the game scoreless. In the end, the game came down to penalty kicks—a kicker versus goalie match-up where the team that scores the most goals in five chances wins.

The coin toss determined China would kick first. Each team scored on its first two penalty kicks, with Xie Huilin and Qui Haiyan tallying for the Chinese, and Carla Overbeck and Joy Fawcett scoring for the U.S.

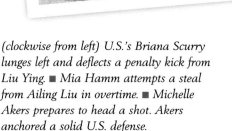

*(clockwise from left) U.S.'s Briana Scurry lunges left and deflects a penalty kick from Liu Ying. ■ Mia Hamm attempts a steal from Ailing Liu in overtime. ■ Michelle Akers prepares to head a shot. Akers anchored a solid U.S. defense.*

(top to bottom) Carla Overbeck sneaks up on China's Ouying Zhang. ■ A young fan wearing a jersey with Mia Hamm's number 9 shows her support. ■ U.S.'s Joy Fawcett attempts a shot on goal. ■ Kristine Lilly fights China's Fan Yunji for possession during regulation play.

But on China's third kick, Scurry blocked Liu Ying's kick, giving the Americans control of the game's destiny. If they could score on their remaining three shots, the Cup would be theirs.

"I knew I just had to make one save the entire game because I knew my teammates would make their shots," Scurry later said, admitting it was instinct that told her to leap left and ricochet the ball out and away from the goal. "I knew if I just got one, we'd probably win."

She was right. Midfielder Lilly followed her game-saving heroics with a kick that put the U.S. up 3 to 2 in the shoot-out. China's Zhang Ouying then evened the score at 3.

That brought up Mia Hamm, whose television commercials with NBA star Michael Jordan helped make her the most recognized player on the U.S. team. But the highest-scoring woman in international soccer history was in a slump this World Cup, having scored only two goals in the tournament. With thousands of young fans wearing jerseys bearing her name, she lived up to expectations by scoring on America's fourth penalty kick.

(clockwise from left) Brandi Chastain swirls her jersey in the air just moments after scoring the game-winning penalty kick. ■ Chastain, center, celebrates with teammates Sara Whalen and Shannon MacMillan. ■ Chastain, left, Julie Foudy, and Carla Overbeck enjoy the medals ceremony. ■ Members of the Chinese team mourn their loss. From left: Ying Liu, Lirong Wen, Ouying Zhang, and Yan Jin.

Sun Wen, China's star player and leading scorer, kept her team alive by scoring its fourth goal. The game now rested on the foot of American Brandi Chastain.

In an exhibition game before the World Cup, Chastain had faced China in a crucial penalty-kick situation. Her shot hit the crossbar and the U.S. lost the game 2 to 1. With redemption on her mind, Chastain set up her kick. As the ball sailed past goalkeeper Gao Hong and hit the right corner of the net, she whipped off her jersey and fell to her knees, clenching her hands in victory.

The ninety thousand-plus fans, many with their faces painted red, white, and blue in support, celebrated as the team captured its second World Cup championship. In the process, the team had invigorated and remodeled the role and perception of women's athletics, embodying skill, strength, poise, and popularity.

# Afterword
## by Wayne Gretzky

Opening this book is like opening a family album. So many of the sights and sounds of my era are contained in here. Reliving these memories is a way of reliving my own life. And I'm not just talking about hockey.

I was a sports nut as a kid, my fascination extending way beyond the ice. Baseball, football, basketball, whatever sport they were showing on TV or broadcasting on the radio, whenever it occurred, you would find me camped out in the living room, enthralled by the feats of my heroes.

On Saturday afternoons, most of my friends would go to the movies in the summertime. Not me. I preferred to stay home and watch the Major League Baseball Game of the Week. Saturday night the entire country came to a halt to watch Hockey Night in Canada.

What was frustrating when I was little was that the game came on at eight and I had to be in bed a little after nine. That's one of the reasons I loved spending the weekend with my grandmother, Mary. I can now reveal that she bent the rules and let me watch the whole game.

Not only that, but she would subject herself to cruel and unusual punishment while we watched the game. I would pretend her legs were the goal posts, and, using a stick she had gotten at a Chicago Blackhawks game, I would try to smack a rubber ball through them. Those legs took a beating, but she never complained. It was all part of watching the games, and probably the best part.

I liked following all sports with my father, Walter. Looking back, I realize that those evenings we spent watching games together formed a bond that has remained strong throughout my life.

I remember at age eleven watching the U.S. lose to the Soviet Union in the controversial gold medal basketball game at the end of the 1972 Olympics. I remember my father was furious. But I also remember my grandfather, Tony, showing no emotion at the outcome. He was from Russia.

It was from that same Olympics that I took away perhaps the most important lesson of my life. I was amazed watching Mark Spitz win gold medal after gold medal in swimming. Seven in all. "How could he do that?" I asked my father. "How could he be so much better than everyone else?"

"Dedication, hard work, total concentration," I was told. Message received. In the years to come, I would try to follow that example driven into my head in my own living room.

I found many other lessons from watching broadcasts of sporting events. Two years later, I was watching Muhammad Ali, whom I consider the athlete of the century, fighting George Foreman in Zaire in the fight known as "The Rumble in the Jungle."

But all I saw as a confused thirteen-year-old was Foreman rumbling forward and Ali tumbling back. I remember wondering what on earth Ali was doing, laying on the ropes getting pummeled. Someone watching the fight with me said, "Wait and see. This guy has a plan." "Yeah," I said, "the plan is that he is going to get crucified." But, as we know, he didn't. When Ali won, I realized how strong and courageous he had to have been to have taken all that punishment in order to become heavyweight champion again. It was another lesson I would carry with me into my own sports career.

Being Canadian, I had my own way of looking at some sporting events in America. While most of those below the border were focused on Secretariat when he won the Triple Crown in 1973, I was focused on the man on his back, jockey Ron Turcotte. Why? Because he was Canadian, of course. I can remember being excited when Nadia Comaneci did so well in the 1976 Olympics. They were in Canada for the first time—instead of halfway around the world—and I felt closer to them.

I can remember time seeming to stand still when Carlton Fisk hit that ball into the night in Boston, waiting along with everyone else to see if it would win the sixth game of the 1975 World Series. I remember laughing at the ending of the Cal–Stanford college football game. It was one of the funniest things I ever saw in sports when that guy ran through the band. That wasn't gang tackling, it was band tackling.

Americans probably won't have this on their list of great moments in sportscasting, but in Canada, we all know where we were when Paul Henderson scored the winning goal for our country in 1972 to win the deciding game against the Soviets in the Canada/Soviet showdown series. I was home because I had talked my dad into letting me miss school, claiming there would be so much noise from the other kids huddled around the television that I wouldn't be able to enjoy the experience. Good old Dad bought my excuse.

In another great sports moment, I cheered in front of the television right along with the Americans. It was 1980 and I was already playing professional hockey, so I knew how good the Soviet Olympic team was that year. For a bunch of American kids to do what they did at Lake Placid—to beat the Soviets—was truly amazing. They beat one of the greatest hockey teams of all time. Al Michaels was right. It was truly a hockey miracle.

I have been immersed in hockey since someone first slipped a pair of skates on my feet, but I have always found time to enjoy other sports. As I look through this book, it stirs many rich memories of those times. You don't have to have played all of these sports yourself to have enjoyed the moments. You need only to have watched and listened.

_Wayne Gretzky_

# Acknowledgments

There are many people to whom I owe special thanks for their contributions of talent, guidance, and encouragement.

I am extremely grateful to Dominique Raccah, President of Sourcebooks, for taking a chance on me two years ago, for her extraordinary vision, and her uncompromising desire to create something truly special. I am proud to be working with her.

Thank you to Todd Stocke, Managing Editor of Sourcebooks, for his exceptional talent and dedication, and his love of sports that kept us all on the right track. Special thanks also to Jennifer Fusco for her patience and her wonderful editing and writing talents.

Thank you to Eric O'Malley and Kirsten Hansen for their artistic skill and tenaciousness in settling for nothing less than the perfect imagery. Also thanks to Carol Davis for expertly coordinating the printing and manufacturing of this compilation.

I want to thank Katie Funk for her meticulous research and fact checking, and Amy Reagan for her tireless persistence in tracking down just the right photo sources.

Thank you to Renee Calomino-Emery, Publicity Director for Sourcebooks, for her creativity and her untiring enthusiasm and passion. Here we go again.

I would like to express my deepest gratitude to Bob Costas for giving *And The Crowd Goes Wild* the most authoritative and eloquent voice possible.

I am extremely grateful to Henry Aaron and Wayne Gretzky, two of the greatest athletes of our time. You offer unique perspectives and I am humbled and honored by your involvement in this book. Thank you for your generosity.

I owe a tremendous debt of gratitude to Louise Argianas from ABC Sports for her generous contribution of insight and encouragement, and her willingness to open doors that I could never have opened without her.

I am also grateful for the opportunity and pleasure of having worked with Deanna O'Toole from CBS Sports, and Marc LaPlace from NBC Sports. Their unceasing willingness to share their knowledge and experience throughout this process was invaluable.

Thank you to Wendy Heller-Stein for her contribution of talent, knowledge, enthusiasm, and unwavering perseverance to make this project as good as it could be.

And thank you to Marc Firestone for his counsel, his encouragement, and most of all, his friendship.

I would like to say a special thank you to Bill

Kurtis, a man for whom I have tremendous admiration. Bill provided the voice for the book that started it all, and changed my life.

I would also like to thank Gene Callihan, a family friend who made the very first phone call on behalf of this book—and got the ball rolling.

I would like to thank Pam Davis, Executive Assistant to Bob Costas, for her skillful coordination that kept us on schedule, and also thanks to Kay Reller for her kind support.

Thank you to Susan Bailey for her invaluable assistance in introducing my book to Henry Aaron, and to Mike Barnett of IMG/Hockey for introducing Wayne Gretzky to this project.

Thank you to Don King, Celia Tuckman, Merry Kay Berke, and Angela Bailey of Don King Productions. And thanks to Max Segal from HBO Sports for his assistance.

Thank you to Ivan Gottesfeld of the MSG Network, Richard Chinitz of ESPN Enterprises, Joy Dellapina from NBA Entertainment, Dina Panto from Major League Baseball Properties Library, Arturo Bermudez of Univision Network, David Hyatt of MRN Radio, Hal Ramey of KCBS Radio, and Paul LaSage of WTMJ Radio, for going above and beyond to make sure they provided the best audio footage.

Thank you to Ethan Orlinsky from Major League Baseball Properties, Dennis Lewin from the NFL, and Adam Silver from the NBA, for allowing their leagues to be included in this book.

I want to thank Laura Zappi of the United States Olympic Committee for permitting the inclusion of broadcasts of the memorable Olympic events.

Thank you to Manu Appelius, for sharing his knowledge of soccer. Thank you to Tom Jordan at Corbis Images, Carolyn McMahon at AP/Wide World Photos, Karen Carpenter at Sports Illustrated, Jim Lee at Allsport Photography, and Larry Schwartz and Arlete Santos at Archive Photo for their determination in providing us with the best possible images.

Thank you to David and Connie Garner; John and Karen Garner; Susan and Tom Wenzel; Jerry, Sandi, and Brian Barnes; and Bonnie and Al Pollan for their love, support, and encouragement throughout. A special thank you to my son J.B. (James) and daughter Jillian for their love and patience. And as always, thank you to my parents, Jim and Betty Garner, for instilling in me the conviction to pursue my dreams.

Finally, I offer my heartfelt gratitude to Jeff Lamont, Dan Kavanaugh, and everyone at Mirage Productions, for their extraordinary support. I could not ask for better partners and friends.

# Photo Credits

All credits listed by page number, in the order indicated on pages.

Every effort has been made to correctly attribute all the materials reproduced in this book.
If any errors have been made, we will be happy to correct them in future editions.

**Page iv** Ed Honowitz/Tony Stone Images **Babe Ruth** 2 Corbis/Bettmann; 3 UPI/Corbis-Bettmann; 4 Kirk Kandle; 5 AP/Wide World Photos, AP/Wide World Photos, Allsport/Hulton Deutsch **Jesse Owens** 6 Archive Photos; 7 Corbis/Hulton-Deutsch Collection; 8 Corbis/Bettmann, Corbis/Bettmann, Corbis/Bettmann; 9 Corbis/Bettmann, Allsport **Joe Louis** 10 AP/Wide World Photos; 11 Corbis/Bettmann; 12 UPI/Corbis-Bettmann, Corbis/Bettmann-UPI, Corbis-Bettmann; 13 Corbis/Bettmann, Corbis/Bettmann, AP/Wide World Photos, Popperfoto **Lou Gehrig** 14 UPI/Corbis-Bettmann; 15 AP/Wide World Photos; 16 Corbis/Bettmann, Corbis/ Bettmann, Corbis/Bettmann; 17 AP/Wide World Photos **Bobby Thomson** 18 AP/Wide World Photos; 19 AP/Wide World Photos; 20 UPI/Corbis-Bettmann, AP/Wide World Photos, UPI/Corbis-Bettmann; 21 UPI/Corbis-Bettmann, Patrick A Burns/New York Times Co./Archive Photos **Don Larsen** 22 AP/Wide World Photos; 23 Corbis Bettmann; 24 AP/Wide World Photos; 25 AP/Wide World Photos, Reuters/Ray Stubblebine/ Archive Photos **Colts vs. Giants** 26 AP/Wide World Photos; 27 AP/Wide World Photos **Wilma Rudolph** 28 AP/Wide World Photos; 29 AP/Wide World Photos, AP/Wide World Photos; 30 AP/Wide World Photos, Archive Photos, AP/Wide World Photos, Allsport/ Hulton Deutsch; 31 Corbis/Bettmann-UPI, Allsport/Hulton Deutsch, UPI/Corbis-Bettmann **Ted Williams** 32 Archive; 33 AP/Wide World Photos; 34 AP/Wide World Photos, AP/Wide World Photos; 35 Archive, AP/Wide World Photos **Bill Mazeroski** 36 Corbis/Bettmann; 37 Corbis/Bettmann, Corbis/Bettmann; 38 Corbis/Bettmann, Corbis/ Bettmann; 39 Corbis/Bettmann, Corbis/Bettmann, Corbis/Charles Harris/Pittsburgh Courier **Wilt Chamberlain** 40 AP/Wide World Photos; 41 AP/Wide World Photos **Billy Mills** 42 AP/Wide World Photos; 43 Corbis/Bettmann-UPI, Archive Photos **Havlicek** 44 Walter Iooss, Jr./Sports Illustrated; 45 AP/Wide World Photos, AP/Wide World Photos **Ice Bowl** 46 AP/Wide World Photos; 47 Corbis/Bettmann; 48 Corbis/Bettmann, Corbis/Bettmann; 49 Corbis/Bettmann, AP/Wide World Photos **Bob Beamon** 50 Allsport; 51 Archive Photos, AP/Wide World Photos **Super Bowl III** 52 Herb Scharfman/Sports Illustrated; 53 W. Ioos/Sports Illustrated; 54 Corbis, Neil Leifer/Sports Illustrated, AP/Wide World Photos; 55 New York Times Co./Archive Photos, Walter Ioos, Jr./Sports Illustrated, Neil Leifer/Sports Illustrated **Miracle Mets** 56 Corbis/Bettmann; 57 Corbis/Bettmann; 58 Corbis/Bettmann, AP/Wide World Photos, AP/Wide World Photos, AP/Wide World Photos; 59 Corbis/Bettman, AP/Wide World Photos, AP/Wide World Photos **Willis Reed** 60 Photography from the lens of George Kalinsky, Major League Graphics; 61 Photography from the lens of George Kalinsky, Major League Graphics, Photography from the lens of George Kalinsky, Major League Graphics **Mark Spitz** 62 AP/Wide World Photos; 63 Archive Photos; 64 Allsport/Hulton Deutsch, Corbis/Bettmann, Archive Photos/Popperfoto; 65 Corbis/Bettmann, AP/Wide World Photos **1972 Olympic Basketball** 66 Corbis/Bettmann-UPI; 67 Popperfoto/Archive Photos; 68 Archive Photos/Popperfoto, AP/Wide World Photos, AP/Wide World Photos; 69 AP/Wide World Photos, AP/Wide World Photos **Immaculate Reception** 70 AP/Wide World Photos; 71 ©Dick Raphael/NFL Photos, ©NFL Photos **Secretariat** 72 Corbis/Jerry Cooke; 73 Sports Illustrated, John Iacono/Sports Illustrated; 74 Neil Leifer/Sports Illustrated, Neil Leifer/Sports Illustrated, Heinz Kluetmeier/Sports Illustrated; 75 Corbis/Jerry Cooke, Corbis/Jerry Cooke **Billie Jean King** 76 Corbis/Bettmann-UPI; 77 Express Newspapers/10767/Archive Photos, Corbis/Bettmann; 78 AP/Wide World Photos, AP/Wide World Photos; 79 UPI/Corbis-Bettmann, Corbis/Bettmann-UPI, Corbis/Bettmann **Hank Aaron** 80 Corbis/Bettmann; 81 AP/Wide World Photos; 82 APA/Archive Photos, Baseball Hall of Fame Library/Major League Baseball Photos; 83 Corbis/Bettmann, AP/Wide World Photos, Corbis/Bettmann **Muhammad Ali** 84 Corbis/Bettmann; 85 Corbis/Bettmann, Allsport/(USOC); 86 UPI/Corbis-Bettmann, Corbis/Bettmann, Allsport/Hulton Deutsch, Corbis/Bettmann; 87 UPI/Corbis-Bettmann, Larry C. Morris/New York Times Co./Archive Photos, Larry C. Morris/New York Times Co./Archive Photos, Barton Silverman/New York Times Co./Archive Photos; 88 Corbis/Bettmann, AP/Wide World Photos, Agence France Presse/Archive Photos; 89 Corbis/Bettmann, UPI/Corbis-Bettmann, Corbis/Bettmann **Carlton Fisk** 90 Corbis/Bettmann; 91 Corbis/Bettmann-UPI, Corbis/Bettmann-UPI; 92 AP/Wide World Photos, AP/Wide World Photos, AP/Wide World Photos; 93 Corbis/Bettmann, AP/Wide World Photos **Nadia Comaneci** 94 Heinz Kluetmeier/Sports Illustrated; 95 Allsport, Corbis/Wally McNamee; 96 Jerry Cooke/Sports Illustrated, AP/Wide World Photos, Neil Leifer/Sports Illustrated; 97 Don Morley/Allsport, Tony Duffy/Allsport, Corbis/Wally McNamee **Magic Johnson vs. Larry Bird** 98 AP/Wide World Photos; 99 Corbis/Bettmann; 100 AP/Wide World Photos, Corbis/Bettmann, Corbis/Bettmann, Corbis/Bettmann; 101 Corbis/Bettmann, Corbis/Bettmann, Corbis/Bettmann, Corbis/Bettmann **1980 Olympic Hockey** 102 Sports Illustrated; 103 Corbis/Bettmann; 104 Corbis/Galen Rowell, Corbis/Bettmann, Corbis/Wally McNamee, AP/Wide World Photos; 105 UPI/Corbis-Bettmann, Corbis/Bettmann, UPI/Corbis-Bettmann **Borg vs. McEnroe** 106 AP/Wide World Photos; 107 Corbis/Bettmann-UPI; 108 Allsport/Tony Duffy, Steve Powell/Allsport; 109 Allsport/Steve Powell, Allsport/Steve Powell, Corbis/Bettmann, UPI/Corbis-Bettmann **The Catch** 110 Walter Iooss, Jr./Sports Illustrated 111 Otto Greule/Allsport, Corbis/Bettmann-UPI **Indy 500** 112 ©IMS Photo; 113 ©IMS/Ron McQueeney; 114 ©IMS/Ron McQueeney, ©IMS Photo; 115 ©IMS/Ron McQueeney, Corbis/Bettmann-UPI **The Play** 116 David Madison; 117 David Madison; 118 Robert B. Stinnett, Robert B. Stinnett, Robert B. Stinnett; 119 Robert B. Stinnett, Robert B. Stinnett **NC State vs. Houston** 120 AP/Wide World Photos; 121 AP/Wide World Photos; 122 AP/Wide World Photos, AP/Wide World Photos; 123 AP/Wide World Photos, AP/Wide World Photos **Richard Petty** 124 Daytona Racing Archives; 125 Daytona Racing Archives, Daytona Racing Archives; 126 Daytona Racing Archives, Daytona Racing Archives, Daytona Racing Archives; 127 Daytona Racing Archives, Daytona Racing Archives, AP/Wide World Photos **Hail Mary** 128 UPI/Corbis-Bettmann; 129 AP/Wide World Photos **Jack Nicklaus** 130 AP/Wide World Photos; 131 AP/Wide World Photos; 132 AP/Wide World Photos, AP/Wide World Photos, AP/Wide World Photos; 133 Corbis/Bettmann-UPI, AP/Wide World Photos **Kirk Gibson** 134 Will Hart/Allsport; 135 Will Hart/Allsport, UPI/Corbis-Bettmann **Douglas vs. Tyson** 136 AP/Wide World Photos; 137 Ken Levine/Allsport; 138 Reuters/Masaharu Hatano/Archive Photos, Reuters/Kimimasa Mayama/Archive Photos, AP/Wide World Photos/Sadayuki Mikami; 139 Reuters/Masaharu Hatano/Archive Photos, AP/Wide World Photos **Carl Lewis** 140 Reuters/Gary Hershorn/Archive Photos; 141 Corbis/Bettmann; 142 Corbis/Neal Preston, Corbis/TempSport; 143 Reuters/Mike Blake/Archive Photos, Corbis/S. Carmona, Reuters/Wolfgang Ratay/Archive Photos, Archive Photos **Wayne Gretzky** 144 AP/Wide World Photos; 145 AP/Wide World Photos, AP/Wide World Photos; 146 AP/Wide World Photos; 147 AP/Wide World Photos, AP/Wide World Photos, AP/Wide World Photos **New York Rangers** 148 AP/Wide World Photos/Ron Frehm; 149 Mike Powell/Allsport; 150 Corbis/Reuters, AP/Wide World Photos/Bill Kostroun, AP/Wide World Photos/Bob Jordan; 151 Reuters/Mike Blake/Archive Photos, Corbis/Reuters **Tiger Woods** 152 Reuters/G. Hershorn/Archive Photos; 153 Reuters/Mike Blake/Archive Photos; 154 Tom Russo/UPI/Corbis, Reuters/John Kuntz/Archive Photos, Reuters/John Kuntz/Archive Photos; 155 Reuters/Mike Blake/Archive Photos, AP/Wide World Photos **Michael Jordan** 156 Scott Cunningham/NBA Photos; 157 Corbis/Bettmann; 158 Corbis/Bettmann, Corbis/Bettmann, Corbis/Bettmann; 159 UPI/Corbis-Bettmann, Reuters/Sue Ogrocki/Archive Photos, Birmingham Barons; 160 AP/Wide World Photos, Corbis/Agence France Presse, Jonathan Daniel/Allsport; 161 John Biever/Sports Illustrated, Corbis/AFP **Men's World Cup Soccer** 162 Allsport/Ben Radford; 163 Allsport/David Leah; 164 Allsport/Clive Brunskill, Allsport/Clive Brunskill, Allsport/Stu Forster; 165 Allsport/Shaun Botterill, Allsport/Stu Forster, Allsport/Ben Radford **Mark McGwire** 166 Allsport; 167 Corbis/Bettmann, AP/Wide World Photos; 168 Reuters/Tim Parker/Archive Photos, Agence France Presse/Corbis-Bettmann, Agence France Presse/Corbis-Bettmann; 169 AP/Wide World Photos, AP/Wide World Photos, Allsport **Women's World Cup Soccer** 170 Reuters/David McNew; 171 AP/Wide World Photos, Allsport; 172 Allsport, Reuters, AP/Wide World Photos, Corbis/AFP; 173 Allsport, AP/Wide World Photos, AP/Wide World Photos, AP/Wide World Photos

# Credits

A project of this magnitude is the result of a team of extraordinarily talented and dedicated individuals. I was fortunate to have assembled the best.

**Text/research editorial team:**
Todd Donoho, writer and editorial consultant, is an award-winning veteran Los Angeles KABC-TV sportscaster and host of *Monday Night Live* for more than a decade. Todd is heard daily in Los Angeles on KLOS-FM's *Mark & Brian* radio show.
Bill Stroum is a writer of screenplays and network radio.
Steve Springer is a sportswriter for the *Los Angeles Times.*

**Audio editorial team:**
Narration written by Mark Rowland, writer/producer of television documentaries.
Wendy Heller-Stein was the research consultant for broadcast footage, rights, and clearances.
Additional audio research services were provided by Michael Dolan and Ted Patterson.

**Audio credits:**
Bob Costas was recorded by Bill Schulenburg, Production Consultants, St. Louis, Missouri.
Audio production engineering by Chris Lindsley.

Some audio segments have been edited for time and content. Archival audio provided by and copyright of:

| | | |
|---|---|---|
| ABC Sports, Inc. | Capitol Sports Network | National Football League |
| CBS Sports, Inc. | KCBS Radio, San Francisco, California | NFL Films, Inc. |
| NBC Sports, Inc. | Los Angeles Kings | NBA Entertainment, Inc. |
| ESPN Classic/ESPN Enterprises | Major League Baseball Properties, Inc. | New York Racing Association |
| All England Lawn Tennis and Croquet Club | MRN Radio, a division of International Speedway Corporation | Madison Square Garden Productions/Fox Sports |
| HBO Sports | | WTMJ Radio, Milwaukee, Wisconsin |
| Dorfman Media Corporation | Michigan State University, G. Robert Vincent Voice Library | United States Olympic Committee |
| ESPN Radio, Pittsburgh, Pennsylvania | | Univision Network |

**Special thanks also to:**

| | | | | |
|---|---|---|---|---|
| Atlanta Braves | Green Bay Packers | New York Knicks | New York Yankees | San Francisco 49ers |
| Boston Celtics | Los Angeles Dodgers | New York Mets | Pittsburgh Steelers | |
| Boston Red Sox | New York Jets | New York Rangers | St. Louis Cardinals | |

The author and publisher would especially like to thank the sportscasters listed below, as well as those we were unable to identify. They brought excitement to these moments, and their words will forever be part of our memories.

| | | | | | |
|---|---|---|---|---|---|
| Tom Manning | Ted Moore | Howard Cosell | Jim McKay | Pat Summerall | Jim Nantz |
| Clem McCarthy | Merle Harmon | Milo Hamilton | Sam Posey | Jack Buck | Andres Cantor |
| Russ Hodges | Sam DeLucca | Dick Stockton | Joe Starkey | Bill White | Phil Rizzuto |
| Bob Wolff | Lindsey Nelson | Cathy Rigby | Wally Ausley | Ray Leonard | Mike Shannon |
| Curt Gowdy | Marv Albert | Dick Enberg | Garry Dornburg | Larry Merchant | Joe Buck |
| Bud Palmer | Frank Gifford | Al Michaels | Eli Gold | Jim Lampley | Chris McKendry |
| Chuck Thompson | Chris Schenkel | Bud Collins | Mike Joy | Tom Hammond | Wendy Gebaur |
| Bill O'Donnell | Keith Jackson | Donald Dell | Barney Hall | Bob Miller | John Paul Dellacamera |
| Bill Campbell | Jack Fleming | Don Klein | Brent Musburger | Sal Messina | |
| Johnny Most | Chick Anderson | Wayne Walker | Vern Lundquist | Ken Venturi | |

**Joe Garner** is the *New York Times* bestselling author of *We Interrupt This Broadcast* and is a twenty-year veteran of the radio business, including eleven years as an executive with Westwood One. His expertise on the media's coverage of major events has been featured on *Weekend Today*, CNN, CBS *Up-to-the-Minute*, and hundreds of radio programs nationwide. *We Interrupt This Broadcast* was also a bestseller in the *Wall Street Journal*, *Publishers Weekly*, and *USA Today*. Garner is also the author of *And The Fans Roared*, featuring over forty more thrilling sports broadcasts.

**Bob Costas** holds twelve Emmy awards—eight as outstanding sports broadcaster, two for writing, one for his late night interview show *Later...with Bob Costas* and one for his play-by-play broadcast of the 1997 World Series. He has been named "National Sportscaster of the Year" seven times by his peers. He has been with NBC Sports since 1979 and has covered every major sport, including the Olympics. Costas is a frequent contributor to NBC as a reporter and interviewer on the network's primetime news magazines.